Soft Skills in Demand
for 2020 Career Readiness

Other Books by Pattie Gibson, Ed.D.

The World of Customer Service
Administrative Office Management
Office Skills

Soft Skills in Demand
for 2020 Career Readiness

Pattie Gibson, Ed.D.

Soft Skills in Demand – for 2020 Career Readiness
by Pattie Gibson, Ed.D.

Published by Pattie Gibson, Ed.D.
7224 S. Sundown Circle
Littleton, CO 80120

www.pattiegibson.com

ISBN 978-1-7327303-0-4

Book and Cover Design by
Beth Foster Editorial & Design

Table of Contents

Preface   i

PART I: Customer Service Soft Skills   1
Chapter 1: The Customer Experience   3
Chapter 2: The Importance of Serving Customers Well   7
Chapter 3: Emotional Intelligence   11

PART II: Communication Soft Skills   15
Chapter 4: Verbal Communication   17
Chapter 5: Active Listening   21
Chapter 6: Nonverbal Communication   25
Chapter 7: Written Communication   29

PART III: Organizational & Leadership Soft Skills   33
Chapter 8: Project Management   35
Chapter 9: Creative Critical Thinking   39
Chapter 10: Relationship Building   43
Chapter 11: The Work Ethic   47

PART IV: Interpersonal Soft Skills   51
Chapter 12: Problem Solving   53
Chapter 13: Team Building/Teamwork   57
Chapter 14: Negotiation   61
Chapter 15: Collaboration   65

PART V: Self-Management Soft Skills   69
Chapter 16: Time Management   71
Chapter 17: Stress Management   75
Chapter 18: Professional Awareness   79

About the Author   83

Preface

Soft Skills in Demand – for 2020 Career Readiness is a "learning book" written by a teacher with more than 30 years of successful classroom- and online-based experience and one-on-one contact instruction. My mentor and most favorite educational methods teacher always reinforced: "Your *best* teachers have an abundance of *learning examples;* and because each student learns differently, be prepared with as many as you can find!" Thank you, Dr. Bob Gryder of ASU days! This sage advice has been valuable in my long career of teaching high school, community college, and university students, but especially while selecting examples and activities for this definitive *2020 Soft Skills* learning book.

The "Skills Gap" is *real* in today's customer-oriented workplace. While technical or hard skills will differ by job description and industry, there are some *universal* soft skills that everyone needs to do well in order to succeed in their chosen careers—be they STEM (Science Technology Engineering and Math) or non-technical occupations. These skills include all aspects of the work setting—completing projects as promised, showing up to work on time, being kind to others, listening well, and solving problems in a timely, fair and effective manner, among others. When soft skills complement on-the-job technical skills, it gets you noticed, appreciated and promoted!

Customers do business with people they like and on whom they can count—it's that simple. Worker behaviors and attitudes that go against kindness, logic, meeting commitments, and efficiency get in the way of good business. Unfortunately, over recent years the importance of these soft skills has been significantly undervalued, or possibly unheeded, as the world of business, government, education, and nonprofits has evolved with the advent and growth of technology's impact, among other cultural changes. For some reason, organizations seem to expect that people *know how to behave* when they show up on the job. Sadly, as consumers and business professionals recognize each day, this is not as present in today's workplace as it should be.

This learning book is designed to bridge the skills gap on a *practical level*, not a theoretical one. At the outset, my personal commitment for this book was threefold: 1) to be affordable for students and everyday workers, 2) to be easy to read and understand with an abundance of learning features and examples that make sense, and 3) to contain the essentials in less than 100 jam-packed pages. Moreover, content would embrace learning features that reinforce and mirror 2020 soft skills thinking, accepted wisdom, and workplace demand. The five-part, 18-chapter focus embraces those goals with topics in these major content areas—soft skills in the areas of customer service, communication, organizational leadership, interpersonal relations, and self management.

One core influence in content development came from the findings of a comprehensive 2018 study conducted by LiveCareer, which states:

- 85 percent of job success is related to well-developed soft skills; whereas, only 15 percent comes from hard skills.
- The soft skills most commonly repeated across all occupations are communication skills, customer service, interpersonal skills, organizational skills, and written communication.
- The study's findings corroborate research conducted by Harvard University, the Carnegie Foundation, and Stanford Research Center.

(Source: "2018 Bridging the Skills Gap: An Analysis of Job Ads and Resumes" by LiveCareer in conjunction with TIRO Communications)

Audience

Soft Skills in Demand – for 2020 Career Readiness can be adapted to multiple learning settings—classrooms, online courses, seminars, workshops, and conference break-out sessions—all of which can use the material in the following ways: lecture form, formal presentations, informal discussions, and assigned readings. Post-secondary schools, corporate training departments, and workforce initiative community programs, in addition to the individual learner, will benefit from its study and use.

- **Post-secondary Schools**. Use as a stand-alone course or a complement to a degree or certificate program. Students will supplement their technical knowledge base or hard skills by acquiring soft skills essential for workplace success and advancement.
- **Corporate Training**. Use for corporate training programs to provide reinforcement of soft skills for apprenticeships, internships, and other professional-development coaching and training activities on the job or in the corporate classroom.
- **Workforce Initiative Community Programs**. Use to prepare new workers or those returning to the workforce with basic soft skills needed by job-seekers to be job-ready, as well as for those desiring to advance in pay or position.

The Learning Book at a Glance

PART I. Customer Service Soft Skills

In Chapters 1–3, the learner is introduced to the basic concepts of customer service. Coverage begins with a description of the "Customer Experience," its purpose and goals, and how a customer is defined. Discussion continues to identify how to serve customers well, then explores the influence a person's emotional intelligence has on providing exemplary service.

PART II. Communication Soft Skills

Chapters 4–7 cover how career success depends predominantly on practicing top-notch communication skills in today's workplace. Of the four essential communication skills, the first addressed is verbal, followed by active listening, continuing with nonverbal or body language, and finally the growing importance of effective written communications.

PART III. Organizational & Leadership Soft Skills

Important organizational and leadership skills needed in the workplace are covered in Chapters 8–11. They are project management, creative critical thinking, relationship building, and the importance of one's work ethic.

PART IV. Interpersonal Soft Skills

Chapters 12–15 teach the basics of personal skills, opening with an understanding of the problem-solving process and how to apply it to business dilemmas requiring decisions. The next section continues with today's emphasis on teambuilding and teamwork. The last two chapters teach negotiation and collaboration as indispensable skills for succeeding in today's global, competitive, and economic workplace.

PART V. Self-Management Soft Skills

Chapters 16-18 cover those essential self-management skills *all* successful workers need to master, including how to effectively manage one's time and stress. The final chapter appropriately covers advancing one's professional awareness. It embraces the importance of continuous learning, and explains how customers and co-workers form impressions of one's professionalism through the application of etiquette, manners, and dress in the workplace.

Comprehensive Learning Features

Because the audience for this book can use its content to work effectively in diverse settings and with learners in most any career—STEM and otherwise—the abundance and variety of the following ten tried-and-true *learning approaches* form the core and attest to the uniqueness of *Soft Skills in Demand – for 2020 Career Readiness*. They are described here.

- **Definitions** begin each chapter to ensure a clear understanding of the soft skill's purpose and its function in the workplace.
- **Quotations** introduce each chapter with thoughts from famous people or historians that prompt and focus interest.
- **Examples** of behaviors follow the definition to clarify how the soft skill is applied by ordinary people each day.
- **Reflection Questions** introduce each of the five soft-skills units to engage learners by suggesting they reflect and make notations about their previous personal experiences.
- **"Keep These Points in Mind"** presents the *fundamental* bulleted learning facts, key points, and critical reminders needed to understand and successfully apply the chapter's content to a job or career.

- **Best Practices** provide real-world examples of actual organizations that demonstrate the chapter's soft skill.
- **Soft Skills Tips** provide brief and practical suggestions from today's workplaces.
- **Choices** provide learners with "what if" work dilemmas that allow them to determine their own actions in the given situation.
- **Activities** provide the learner opportunities to *apply* chapter content to solve or reflect on workplace encounters.
- **Further Research and Pretest Links** provide sources to continue investigating and researching the chapter's content. Included also are links to *free* websites where learners can assess their level of proficiency in the soft skill either prior or subsequent to studying the chapter material.

Related Products

- **E-book** is available for reading an electronic version of the printed book.
- **Audiobook** is read by the author and suitable to serve as comprehensive course materials for either online delivery or face-to-face instruction, or as an individual studying method preferred by learners.
- **Author's website, www.pattiegibson.com**, provides book-order links, contact forms, and other resources.

Acknowledgments

I would like to thank family and friends, as well as current and former colleagues and students, for their valuable suggestions and comments throughout the development of this learning book. A very special note of appreciation to Beth Foster for her ongoing attention to *editing catches* (that I missed!), and her forthright honesty when offering really good suggestions to improve each revision cycle and overall design of the book. Developing this learning book has been a fun and truly gratifying venture for me! If it impacts today's workplace in such a way that it becomes more kind to others, more efficient, and more informed, I will feel very pleased.

Pattie Gibson, Ed.D.
September 2018

PART I
Customer Service Soft Skills

Chapter 1
The Customer Experience

Chapter 2
The Importance of Serving Customers Well

Chapter 3
Emotional Intelligence

Part I—Customer Service Reflection Question

Think of the last time you dined out or the last time you purchased an important home item that required interaction with a salesperson. With that situation in mind, what do you remember the most: The food, or the service? Using the product at home, or the service? Jot down some of your thoughts about this experience.

CHAPTER 1
The Customer Experience

"We see our customers as invited guests to a party, and we are the hosts. It's our job to make every important aspect of the customer experience a little bit better."

–Jeff Bezos, CEO, Amazon.com

✔ SOME EXAMPLES OF A GOOD CUSTOMER EXPERIENCE

- Thanking a customer for his business by sending a note or an e-mail message.

- Inviting the customer to contact you with any additional questions or concerns about products or service.

- Meeting a commitment you made to contact the customer to arrange for a free home delivery of her recent replacement order.

✎ Activity 1.1   Answers available at end of chapter.

Have you remained loyal to a particular brand or business over the past three years?

- **?** If so, list two elements of your overall customer experience that produced this loyalty.

The Customer Experience

The product of an interaction between an organization and a customer over the duration of their relationship.

↑ Choices 1.1

You are asked to train a new employee in your department.

- **?** What is one surefire "success strategy" you have used when satisfying customer concerns that you could provide this person?

- **?** Why do you think this particular strategy works so well for you?

Answers available at end of chapter.

⚠ KEEP THESE POINTS IN MIND DURING THE CUSTOMER EXPERIENCE

A good customer experience means that the individual's interactions during *all* points of contact match or exceed the individual's expectations. At each touch point with customers, let your positive attitude shine through and thank them sincerely. Recognize that in the end, customers want their needs addressed by a competent, caring person who can resolve their concerns.

When handling irate customers, try extra hard to:
- Show them that the issue is important to you by sincerely saying, "Thank you for bringing this matter to our attention."
- Apologize *at least* twice, with three times being better—once on hearing the problem, and again after finding a solution.
- Express a sense of urgency and ownership regarding the customer's concern by saying, "I'll take care of this right away."
- Use appropriate responses during exchanges with customers like "Yes," Okay," and "I see."
- Clarify your understanding of the customer problem and use effective listening techniques, including:
  - *Paraphrasing*—Repeat back what was said, using different words for clarification
  - *Summarizing*—Recap points discussed
  - *Questioning*—Ensure clarity on major concerns

Keep in mind that customers often leave and go to a competitor due to:
- Unhappiness with delivery, service, or price.
- Disapproval of unanticipated changes.
- Improper handling of a complaint.
- Feelings of being taken for granted.

As a further reminder, service professionals:
- Always remain courteous, even if the customer is not.
- Avoid using negative and controlling words (e.g., You can't…; It's our policy not to…).
- Give verbal clues (e.g., I see…; Yes, I understand…) and maintain good eye contact to show you are actively listening.
- Use probing skills wisely (e.g., What exactly do you mean by quality issues? Please give an example of the poor service you received.).
- Promise to follow up on any unresolved issues or commitments, then do it.
- Speak to irate customers using a softer tone of voice with the hope they will match your tone during responses.

EXAMPLES OF BEST PRACTICES

Customer Service at Successful Companies
www.business.com/articles/fortune-500-customer-service-lessons *Accessed 6/8/2018*

Netflix
When customers have a problem that needs fixing, Netflix offers a range of solutions that help customers help themselves. Netflix's Help Center includes an extensive knowledge base with a wide selection of online self-service options, plus a toll-free phone number and an e-mail address. There's also a search option. In more complicated situations, live chat delivers a personable reply with a one-minute response time.

Southwest Airlines
Southwest Airlines focuses on employee satisfaction above all else. Within defined boundaries, the company empowers employees to use their initiative to solve problems. Making employees feel responsible for the airline's success helps create an environment that encourages staff to go the extra mile for customers. By providing the type of top-tier service rarely found in its industry, Southwest sets itself apart from the competition.

 ## Soft Skills Tip 1.1
When you are trying to understand a customer's situation, remember that the *problem* is the enemy, not you. In other words, don't take the interaction personally, and strive to be a professional at all times.

 ## Activity 1.2

Answers available at end of chapter.

A woman had recently bought a baby mattress for her newborn from The Little Store. She was very dissatisfied with the quality of the product after using it only a short time. She felt the mattress was made with unsafe materials and was concerned for her baby's health and safety. When the customer told the new sales associate, Melissa, that she wanted her money back, Melissa said pleasantly, "I will have to check with the store manager to see if we can take back this used mattress for a full refund or not." At that point, the customer lost her temper and said, "What is the issue? Why do you have to check with anyone at all?"

? Evaluate the actions of the customer and of Melissa in this situation. What did Melissa do well, and what are some errors she inadvertently made?

 **FURTHER RESEARCH AND PRETEST LINKS**

Customer Service Institute of America (CSIA)
https://www.serviceinstitute.com

Pretest by ProProfs Quiz MakeR: The Customer Service Challenge Quiz
https://www.proprofs.com/quiz-school/story.php?title=customer-service-exam

Answers to Chapter 1 Exercises

Note: Though answers may vary due to experience and previous training, the following are suggested responses.

Activity 1.1: In response to whether you have remained loyal to a particular brand or business over the past three years, you could say that some reasons that produced this loyalty are friendliness, customer-oriented, great service, have products on shelves, helpful when answering questions.

Activity 1.2: When evaluating the actions of the customer, keep in mind that she is spurred by concern for her child and is probably emotional when it comes to her child's safety. For that reason, Melissa needs to listen very carefully, demonstrate agreement with the customer, and immediately state that she is happy to take care of the customer with a replacement mattress.

Choices 1.1: For a success strategy, students could mention the following behaviors: listening well, good eye contact with a customer, friendly service, follow-through when solving customer problems, etc.

NOTES:

CHAPTER 2
The Importance of Serving Customers Well

"There is only one boss—the customer. And he can fire everybody in the company, from the chairman on down, simply by spending his money somewhere else."
–Sam Walton, Founder of Wal-Mart

✓ SOME EXAMPLES OF SERVING CUSTOMERS WELL

- Offering a warm and sincere greeting to customers when they enter the business.

- Taking note of repeat customers and gathering details on their purchase history among other things; then being sure to *only* use this customer data to serve them better.

- Finding a way to connect with customers through things you have in common.

 Activity 2.1 <small>Answers available at end of chapter.</small>

Think about any job you've had. In what ways were you an "internal customer" in that company?

? Recall the colleagues who made your work easier or who helped you *look good* upon completion of a task.

? What happens in organizations that downplay or do not recognize the critical importance of serving internal customers?

? In your opinion, which is more important—the internal customer, or the external customer? Explain.

Serving Customers Well

The process of satisfying the customer, relative to the product or service, in whatever way the customer defines his or her need, and having that service delivered with efficiency, compassion, and sensitivity.

⚡Choices 2.1

? In your opinion, is it ever acceptable to stand your ground with a customer and not give in to his or her demands? Explain your position by citing an example.

? Also, given the three customer turnoffs mentioned on Page 10, which one is the most critical to avoid happening to a customer? Explain your choice.

<small>Answers available at end of chapter.</small>

⚠ KEEP THESE POINTS IN MIND WHILE SERVING CUSTOMERS WELL

Exceptional customer service occurs when customers get *more* than they expected from a service provider. As a result, service is an important mindset that defines each company's culture. A top-notch organization ensures that excellent customer service is pervasive, is visible to others, and is *everyone's* responsibility by doing the following:

● Always remain courteous, even if the customer is not.

● Always recognize that if a company doesn't take care of its customers, some other company will.

● Honor those customers who have high expectations, because they make a business better. The secret is to use the situation as an opportunity to both maximize customer retention and improve customer service.

● When managing customer complaints:
  ◆ Admit immediately any mistake on your part.
  ◆ Stand behind your promises.
  ◆ Handle criticism tactfully.
  ◆ Stress what you *can* do, not what you cannot do.

Identify distinctive actions and behaviors among your customers (internal or external, quiet or vocal) to better understand their unique needs and, more importantly, how best to serve them. For example:

● **Internal/External**
  ◆ *Internal customers* include employees or departments in a company that rely on colleagues to provide the support they need to serve their own internal and external customers.
  ◆ *External customers* include those whose needs we traditionally think of serving—those who purchase and use a company's products and services.

● **Extreme Customers—Quiet and Vocal**
  ◆ *Quiet customers* think: "The business must know about this problem already, so I'm just going to stay quiet"; they then *behave* by going away quietly because they hate conflict. (Always remember that a lost customer is difficult and costly to get back.)
  ◆ *Vocal customers* get angry and think: "No one is listening to me." They can become abusive, personal, and even threatening to service providers, who will need to strive especially hard to maintain their self-awareness, tact, and diplomacy throughout the *entire* exchange.

(continued on Page 10)

EXAMPLE OF BEST PRACTICES
Serving Customers Well
http://www.ritzcarlton.com/en/about/gold-standards
Accessed 6/11/2018

Part of what makes the **Ritz-Carlton Hotel Company** highly regarded are the high standards they have set as the foundation upon which they operate. In addition to employees being empowered to spend up to $2,000 to resolve a customer problem without consulting a supervisor, guest service agents also observe these hotel service values:

1. I am always responsive to the expressed and unexpressed needs of our guests.
2. I am empowered to create unique, memorable, and personal experiences for our guests.
3. I own and immediately resolve guest problems.
4. I create a work environment of teamwork and service so that the needs of our guests and team members are met.
5. I have the opportunity to continuously learn and grow.
6. I am involved in the planning of the work that affects me.
7. I am proud of my professional appearance, language, and behavior.

It is easy to see why Ritz-Carlton's motto is "We are Ladies and Gentlemen serving Ladies and Gentlemen."

Soft Skills Tip 2.1

In delivering great customer service, create a customer experience that is unique to that person and isn't the same as the next customer's.

Choices 2.2

? What best reflects your views, in general, when dealing with customer service issues:
 ◆ "I tell the whole truth, all the time," *or*
 ◆ "I play by the rules, but I bend them to my company's advantage whenever I can."

? Which view speaks to who you are in a service situation, and why?

Answers available at end of chapter.

Activity 2.2

Answers available at end of chapter.

Do you, as a customer, use social media tools (e.g., Yelp) on a regular basis to evaluate your customer service experiences?

? If so, which tools do you use most frequently when sharing a positive or negative customer-service evaluation?

? In your opinion, what effect do these evaluations have on your returning for future purchases—in the short term and in the long term?

KEEP THESE POINTS IN MIND (continued from Page 8)

Finally, keep in mind that there are three **customer turnoffs** organizations should attempt to prevent and always avoid:

- **Value turnoffs:** The company failed to meet the customer's *quality* expectations. (Example: "I didn't get my money's worth.")
- **System turnoffs:** The customer became irritated with *how* the company delivered their service. (Example: "Their voicemail system makes me crazy! I can't get to the right person to solve my problem.")
- **People turnoffs:** The customer experienced lack of courtesy or an indifferent attitude by the service professional. (Example: "She was downright rude to me!")

 FURTHER RESEARCH LINK

International Customer Service Association (ICSA)
http://icsatoday.org

Answers to Chapter 2 Exercises

Note: Though answers may vary due to experience and previous training, the following are suggested responses.

Activity 2.1: Organizations that downplay or do not recognize the critical importance of serving internal customers lose both internal and external customers. Some problems that often arise involve a lack of support between and among colleagues and the rumblings of office politics. Whether or not one category of customer is more important than the other *just depends*, and the reasons will vary depending on personal experience.

Activity 2.2: Answers will vary relative to usage of and experience with the different social media tools, such as Yelp, Facebook, and Instagram.

Choices 2.1: *First part:* In general, it is advisable to try to find a win-win compromise when solving customer concerns. *Second part:* Generally, it is a people problem that is more difficult to isolate and solve rather than value and system turnoff problems.

Choices 2.2: Student responses will differ depending on previous experiences with "truth" as they so define it and with "rules" being absolute or not. Should be a lively discussion.

NOTES:

CHAPTER 3
Emotional Intelligence

"Unexpressed emotions will never die. They are buried alive and will come forth later in uglier ways."

–Sigmund Freud, Founder of Psychoanalysis

✔ SOME EXAMPLES OF EMOTIONAL INTELLIGENCE

- Being angry with someone may motivate you to say something you will regret later; but by thinking rationally *before speaking*, you will become more emotionally intelligent.

- Remembering that even though you've had a tough day at work, there is no reason to take it out on your children or significant other when you get home.

- Practicing emotional intelligence each day not only helps you be a better employee; more importantly, it helps you be the best role model for team members to emulate.

 Activity 3.1   Answers available at end of chapter.

Spencer and Lauren were asked to share an office, but it became obvious that the two did not have compatible work styles. For example, Spencer chattered constantly, so Lauren made a point of using ear plugs. This was the last straw for Spencer—he blew up and stormed to their manager's office.

? Describe the kinds of emotions Spencer and Lauren are experiencing.

? How might they each have behaved differently?

? How might they improve their relationship, given there is no additional office space in their area?

Emotional Intelligence

The ability to recognize and understand what others are experiencing emotionally and what motivates others to action.

⬆ Choices 3.1

Emotional intelligence differs from how we think of intellectual ability, in that emotional intelligence is *learned*—not acquired. This learning can take place at any time in life, so the social and emotional skill set known as emotional intelligence is something we can all have.

? How have you learned the principles of emotional intelligence (e.g., experience, school, family, sports, clubs)?

? Explain how you would rate your use of this skill in both your personal and work lives.

Answers available at end of chapter.

⚠ KEEP THESE POINTS IN MIND ABOUT EMOTIONAL INTELLIGENCE

The four elements of emotional intelligence are:

- **Self-awareness:** You recognize your own emotions and understand how they affect your thoughts and behavior.
- **Self-management:** You are able to control impulsive feelings and behaviors, manage your emotions in healthy ways, take initiative, follow through on promises, and adapt to new events.
- **Social awareness:** You understand the emotions, needs, and concerns of other people. You pick up on emotional cues and feel comfortable socially.
- **Relationship management:** You know how to develop and maintain good relationships, communicate clearly, inspire and influence others, work well on a team, and manage conflict.

Mindfulness is related to emotional intelligence in that it creates an awareness of what is happening within and around you *right now*. As such, it can improve your focus and help break disruptive behavior patterns before you act.

Finally, remember to:

- Always remain courteous, even if the customer is not.
- Ask questions instead of criticizing. Asking questions helps customers feel their concerns/issues are important.
- Live in the present. There is no sense thinking or worrying about what has happened in the past or what might happen tomorrow.
- Try to accept change. Learn to grow with the pace of changes that are happening around you.
- Take time out for yourself—it's important to make time occasionally *just for you*.

 **Activity 3.2**

Answers available at end of chapter.

Julie had spent hours preparing her presentation for the next team meeting, which would address the question of how future products would impact sales. She had practiced extensively and knew she was good to go. However, when she got to the third slide, she was interrupted—rudely, she thought—by Bill, a former manager of her department. Bill said, "We don't need to cover that now—we have more important issues to cover in the next hour or so." Surprised that no one opposed Bill's statement, Julie felt awful and returned to her seat. **(continued next page)**

EXAMPLE OF BEST PRACTICES
Emotional Intelligence
https://liveboldandbloom.com/02/self-awareness-2/
emotional-intelligence-workplace *Accessed 6/7/2018*

In the workplace, empathetic employees have the ability to identify with and understand the feelings, wants, needs, and viewpoints of those around them, which improves their emotional intelligence with others. They are able to listen well, relate easily to others, and avoid stereotyping or judging too quickly.

Here are some useful actions to improve empathy:

- Consciously try to view situations from the other person's point of view. Recognize that we are all working from the knowledge and experience we have—rather than judging the person as right or wrong or good or bad.

- Examine your own attitude and motives. Do you just want to be right, to prove a point or win the argument, or are you truly interested in the best outcome or solution, even if it's not yours?

- Practice the Golden Rule: In every situation, treat others the way you would want to be treated.

 # Soft Skills Tip 3.1
Being mindful means being aware of the *present only*. It has nothing to do with thinking about what you have to do tomorrow, or what you should have done yesterday.

Activity 3.2 (continued)

Answers available at end of chapter.

? Have you ever experienced a situation where you were embarrassed beyond belief? If so, how did you handle it?

? If you were Julie, what actions would you have taken or what might you have said in order to continue your presentation?

? What do you think motivated Bill to speak as he did to Julie?

? If you were on the team, would you have spoken up and countered Bill's statement? Why, or why not?

 **FURTHER RESEARCH AND PRETEST LINKS**

Consortium for Research on Emotional Intelligence in Organizations
http://www.eiconsortium.org

Pretest by Institute for Health and Human Potential
https://www.ihhp.com/free-eq-quiz

Answers to Chapter 3 Exercises

Note: Though answers may vary due to experience and previous training, the following are suggested responses.

Activity 3.1: It is obvious that Spencer and Lauren are having difficulty adapting as space-mates. Perhaps the manager or they themselves didn't start out by exploring how they would manage with such different work styles. The point being, emotional intelligence is needed in this situation—both Spencer and Lauren need to take a breath, step back, and discuss what they each can do to make this situation work.

Activity 3.2: This incident should have been avoided at all costs, but clearly it was not. Being respectful and considerate to Julie was not what Bill demonstrated, and he should have. Students' responses to the questions will vary, but should promote good discussion especially if they have encountered a similar uncomfortable situation.

Choices 3.1: Student responses will vary.

NOTES:

PART II
Communication Soft Skills

Chapter 4
Verbal Communication

Chapter 5
Active Listening

Chapter 6
Nonverbal Communication

Chapter 7
Written Communication

Part II—Communication Reflection Question

Reflect on your communication skills relative to being able to effectively get your point across. With your communication skills in mind, how would you rank yourself (1 through 4, with 1 being your strongest skill) on each of the following?

_____Verbal Communication
_____Active Listening
_____Nonverbal Communication
_____Written Communication

? What is your strongest skill, and what can you attribute that to (e.g., experience, training, comes naturally, etc.)?

? What is your least strong skill, and why do you think so?

CHAPTER 4
Verbal Communication

"Say a little and say it well."
–Irish Proverb

✅ SOME EXAMPLES OF VERBAL COMMUNICATION

- Speaking over the phone to a business colleague.
- Sharing information about your team's progress during a department meeting.
- Making a PowerPoint presentation about this year's corporate goals at the January "kick-off" meeting.

 **Activity 4.1** <small>Answers available at end of chapter.</small>

Do some research and locate a Toastmasters Club that meets in your community. You might already know someone who is an active member whom you can ask, or you can visit the organization's website.

? What occurs during regular Toastmasters meetings?

? Where do they meet, and how often do they get together?

? Is there a cost to join? If so, what is it?

? Can you attend a meeting for informational purposes prior to joining Toastmasters Club?

Verbal Communication

The type of oral communication wherein the message is transmitted through the spoken word.

 **Choices 4.1**

When speaking to others, each of us has a choice to avoid using rude and insensitive statements. Read and think about each of the following statements, then provide a more appropriate response.

Hint: Use "I" statements rather than "you" statements. For example, instead of saying "Wait here" to a customer, instead say "I'll just be a moment. Would you mind waiting here?")

Rephrase these statements to sound more customer-oriented:
"You didn't do this right."
"Why are you so upset?"
"What's your problem?"

<small>Answers available at end of chapter.</small>

⚠ KEEP THESE POINTS IN MIND
ABOUT VERBAL COMMUNICATION

- Speaking your thoughts clearly requires extra thought and concentration as you refrain from monopolizing the conversation or interrupting others.
- Exercise effort to speak calmly even when you are feeling stressed.
- Paraphrase, or repeat back, using different words to show understanding.
- Provide concrete examples to explain ideas.
- Explain a difficult situation without getting angry.
- Avoid verbally belittling or making fun of a colleague or customer. It is just not the right thing to do, and it certainly is not funny to the receiver.
- Make sure that not only your words, but your tone, gestures, facial expressions, and body language go with the conversation to ensure clear, accurate, considerate communication.
- Slow down when speaking to older people; articulate words clearly and avoid using slang expressions.

In addition, verbal communication is critical to one's success because:
- It occurs in many different settings including training sessions, presentations, group meetings, performance appraisals, one-on-one discussions, sales pitches, and consulting engagements, among others.
- It is key to an organization's success because it improves business relationships, increases productivity, and decreases errors.
- In the workplace, employees experience an increase in morale, productivity, and commitment if they are encouraged to communicate up and down the organization's leadership chain.
- Clear and transparent one-on-one verbal communication is vital to effective company operations.
- Maintaining eye contact while talking with colleagues can help you determine if they are actively listening to you.

 **Activity 4.2**

Answers available at end of chapter.

Neal Edwards enjoys his reputation at the Haynes Bookstore customer service department. He takes calls from customers that others don't want to deal with. Sometimes when on the phone with a customer, he asks coworkers to come near his desk to hear his side of the *argument*—often getting loud and belligerent and later boasting of "winning." **(continued next page)**

Verbal Communication

EXAMPLE OF BEST PRACTICES
Verbal Communication
https://mediacenter.toastmasters.org/2017-08-09-Fortune-500-Companies-Develop-Employees-Through-Toastmasters *Accessed 6/11/2018*

More than half of all Fortune 500 companies now offer in-house Toastmasters Clubs to help employees become better communicators and leaders. Amazon, Bank of America, Boeing, Coca-Cola, Ford, Google, and Verizon are among the industry giants that have found the Toastmasters International program effective for staff development and an asset for the bottom line.

"Every Google employee has to be a good communicator because they have to work with multiple teams and often in multiple geographies around the world," says Gopi Kallayil, Chief Evangelist for Brand Marketing at Google. "Good communication is a key driver for success at Google. Joining Toastmasters has fundamentally pivoted my life and is one of the best investments I have made in my professional growth."

Toastmasters' communication and leadership programs teach employees how to:
- Conduct effective meetings
- Practice time management
- Enhance their listening skills
- Sharpen their presentation skills
- Boost team collaboration
- Guide successful teams

 ## Soft Skills Tip 4.1
You will find that asking open-ended questions (*questions requiring more than a "yes" or "no" answer*) during a conversation stimulates dialog and greatly influences the clarity of the message.

Activity 4.2 (continued)
Answers available at end of chapter.

Things have changed, however, and Neal is now in trouble with management because of a recent incident. A loyal five-year customer who spoke to Neal on the phone last week contacted owner Chuck Haynes and told him she will no longer buy from his bookstore.

? Why has Neal's behavior continued?

? As his coworker, would you have any responsibility to report Neal's aggressive communication style with customers to Mr. Haynes?

 **FURTHER RESEARCH AND PRETEST LINKS**

Toastmasters International

https://www.toastmasters.org

Pretest by ProProfs Quiz Maker

https://www.proprofs.com/quiz-school/story.php?title=verbal-communication-skills-quiz

Answers to Chapter 4 Exercises

Note: Though answers may vary due to experience and previous training, the following are suggested responses.

Activity 4.1: Toastmasters Clubs generally are open to all interested parties and encourage interested people to attend a first club meeting as an observer. Meetings are typically twice a month and are scheduled around the noon hour, lasting anywhere from one to two hours. Dues are generally around $100 per year and there typically is a new member fee, usually around $25. Consult the local Toastmasters website for more up-to-date information.

Activity 4.2: Neal's behavior has continued because he has been allowed to be rude to customers. Students' responses will vary; but in general, coworkers have a responsibility to report Neal's behavior because customers should not be treated in this way under any circumstances.

Choices 4.1: Examples of responses are:

- This can be confusing. May I show you how it is done?
- It is clear you are upset, and I'm sorry. How can I help?
- I am sorry you haven't found a solution to this problem. Perhaps I can help?

NOTES:

CHAPTER 5
Active Listening

"I remind myself every morning: Nothing I say this day will teach me anything. So if I'm going to learn, I must do it by listening."

–Larry King, American TV Host

✅ SOME EXAMPLES OF ACTIVE LISTENING

- Listening intently to a councilmember discussing personal-safety concerns at a city council meeting.

- Summarizing what your team said during a weekly meeting and asking them if you heard their comments correctly.

- Restating specific areas in which your supervisor indicates you might improve.

 **Activity 5.1**   Answers available at end of chapter.

Jim, a guest services agent at a top resort in the city, is listening intently to respond to an international traveler's question. The guest is asking for directions to a popular restaurant in the area. Although Jim has repeated the driving instructions several times, the traveler still does not seem to understand how to drive there. Jim is wondering what he should do next.

? What are two creative steps Jim or his hotel can take to prevent this frustrating communication situation from happening to other guests in the future—especially with the increase of international travelers?

Active Listening

The ability to pay close attention to what the other person is saying, ask clarifying questions, and rephrase what the person says to ensure total understanding of the communiqué.

 **Choices 5.1**

Suppose you work with a person who, after serving certain ethnic customers, makes comments about how slow to understand he feels this ethnic group is, and how he would prefer that you take care of these customers in the future, instead of him.

? Would this bother you enough to let your co-worker know how you feel about his service attitude?

? What would you say to him?

Answers available at end of chapter.

⚠ KEEP THESE POINTS IN MIND ABOUT ACTIVE LISTENING

- While many think communication skills are all about speaking, being a good listener is just as important. Listening shows interest and respect for others.

- Active listeners are patient. They graciously accept natural pauses and short periods of silence during the conversation.

- The three main types of listening most common in interpersonal communication are:
  - *Informational*: Listening to learn
  - *Critical*: Listening to evaluate and analyze
  - *Empathetic*: Listening to understand feelings or emotions

- Most people have difficulty listening effectively…
  - when dealing with conflict or emotionally charged topics or persons.
  - when they are feeling anxious, fearful, or angry.
  - when criticism is being directed at them.

- Avoid these communication roadblocks:
  - Even if your intention is to be supportive, don't judge or criticize another person.
  - Be aware that when you respond with a command or an order about what someone should do, it implies that the person is not competent to judge or act independently.
  - Concentrate fully by engaging with what is being said rather than just *passively* hearing the message of the speaker.
  - Clarify what you heard the other person say by paraphrasing what was said in your own words.

 **Activity 5.2**

Answers available at end of chapter.

Over the next week or so, get together with fellow students, work colleagues, or teammates and do the following activity:

1. Break into pairs consisting of persons A and B.
2. The A person is asked to discuss for three minutes, using no notes, one of these topics: their favorite food, their favorite job of all time, or a family member they truly admire and why.
3. The B person stays quiet and just listens. Then he or she recaps what person A said in one minute—using no notes.

? What was the result of the exchange? Did it demonstrate that Person B listened actively and was able to recall most of what Person A said? Reflect on the results from a learning standpoint.

EXAMPLE OF BEST PRACTICES
Active Listening
http://www.vault.com/blog/networking/8-actions-to-be-an-exceptional-listener *Accessed 7/19/2018*

Most people consider themselves to be good listeners, finding it hard to admit otherwise. Active listening is the single most important communication skill in the business world, where it is valued more highly than speaking. We spend 70 to 80 percent of each day engaged in communication, with over half that time devoted to listening—yet we struggle to do it effectively. Because we hear speech at a rate of 500–1,000 words per minute, and only speak 125–175 words per minute, we become easily bored, distracted, and inattentive.

Here are a couple of ways to stop talking and start listening:

- Stop competing for your turn to talk, and simply listen. Deliberately concentrate your focus on the speaker, maintaining natural eye contact, and tune in to the speaker's facial expressions and body language. Clear your mind and focus on the message.

- Active listening is more than just hearing what someone says; it's about the desire to understand what someone is trying to convey. Mindtools, a career skills development group, reported that people only remember 25 to 50 percent of what they hear, meaning we pay attention to less than half of what someone says. By using words of encouragement such as "I see" and "Go on," we can boost our ability to retain conversational details.

 ## Soft Skills Tip 5.1

In a sense, giving a person your undivided attention while listening is the purest act of respect you can offer. Simply knowing that another person has listened well and understood is empowering.

 ## Soft Skills Tip 5.2

Listening doesn't always mean agreeing. What is important when actively listening is to be attentive and engaged in such a way that the speaker maintains dignity.

 # FURTHER RESEARCH AND PRETEST LINKS

International Listening Association

https://www.listen.org/

Pretest by ThoughtCo.

https://www.thoughtco.com/listening-test-are-you-a-good-listener-31656

Answers to Chapter 5 Exercises

Note: Though answers may vary due to experience and previous training, the following are suggested responses.

Activity 5.1: Jim and the hotel could take the following measures to avoid future communication issues relative to directions: Keep simple written directions at the front desk for the most popular attractions in town, offer shuttle service to and from the hotel, and make detailed maps available at no charge.

Activity 5.2: Student responses will vary, but the key takeaway is that Person B must listen actively by focusing on the total message provided by Person A.

Choices 5.1: If the situation is making you uncomfortable, then yes, have that conversation—including brainstorming together some success strategies for how to work with that particular customer.

NOTES:

CHAPTER 6
Nonverbal Communication

"The most important thing in communication is hearing what isn't said."
Peter Drucker, Management Consultant and Author

✔ SOME EXAMPLES OF NONVERBAL COMMUNICATION

- Maintaining consistent eye contact demonstrates interest and sincerity.

- Touching someone gently on the shoulder shows empathy when that person is getting emotional.

- Squeezing of the hands, fingers, etc., often indicates that someone is nervous or overly anxious.

 **Activity 6.1**   Answers available at end of chapter.

Of all the elements that constitute body language—eye contact, voice, smile, posture, gestures—which three would you describe as the most important to be aware of when serving customers?

? Explain with an example from a past experience why you chose those three elements of body language.

Nonverbal Communication

Body language, such as gestures, movements, and mannerisms by which a person communicates to send the full message to others.

 **Choices 6.1**

A manager says he is very interested in receiving an update from you regarding your team's meeting the previous day. However, while you try to outline the team's most recent actions and discussion points, he reads his e-mail, accepts incoming phone calls—yet, motions you to keep talking.

? How would this exchange make you feel?

? How would you handle the situation?

Answers available at end of chapter.

⚠ KEEP THESE POINTS IN MIND ABOUT NONVERBAL COMMUNICATION

- A substantial portion of our communication is nonverbal. We respond to many nonverbal or body cues and behaviors each day, including postures, facial expressions, eye gaze, gestures, and tone of voice.

- To really understand the full meaning of a message, pay special attention to a person's body language, because nonverbal cues are more immediate, instinctive, and uncontrolled than verbal expressions. As such, they bring attitudes and feelings out into the open.

- From our facial expressions to our body movements, the things we *don't* say still convey volumes of information.

- Keep in mind that nonverbal details reveal *who* we are and impact *how* we relate to other people, oftentimes without our even realizing it.

- Evaluate your own body language from time to time. For example, how would you rate your nonverbal communication skills? **Do you…**
  - lean slightly forward to indicate interest?
  - listen carefully, and not interrupt?
  - modulate your vocal tone to punctuate key points?
  - pay attention to your conversation, and observe how others react to your statements?

- Be aware that clothing, accessories, hairstyles, perfumes, tattoos, piercings, and other factors affecting our appearance are also types of nonverbal communication that send first impressions to others.

EXAMPLE OF BEST PRACTICES

Nonverbal Communication

https://money.usnews.com/money/blogs/outside-voices-careers/articles/2016-04-05/5-tips-to-improve-nonverbal-communication-at-meetings *Accessed 6/6/2018*

When giving a presentation or directing a meeting, all eyes will be on you, so it's extra important to make sure you convey a sense of professionalism. Your appearance, in several areas, communicates a message.

While standards vary depending on your industry, make sure your clothing is pressed and "neutral." You want attendees to pay attention to the information you present, not get distracted by what you are wearing.

However, this doesn't mean you can't let your personality show through. Wearing a small, non-distracting accessory—such as a special tie, a scarf, or jewelry—is acceptable. Just keep it to a minimum.

Finally, ensure that not only your clothes are professional, but your hair looks clean and well-cut as well.

 ## Soft Skills Tip 6.1

In general, try to avoid talking excessively with your hands, as it can appear to some as unprofessional and unpolished.

 ## Soft Skills Tip 6.2

If someone's words do not match their nonverbal behaviors, you should pay careful attention!

Activity 6.2 — Answers available at end of chapter.

? Do you agree with the statement "Actions speak louder than words"?

? In what ways does this thought apply to your overall communication skills and the manner in which you interact with others in the workplace?

# FURTHER RESEARCH AND PRETEST LINKS

National Communication Association

https://www.natcom.org/about-nca/what-nca

Pretest by ProProfs Quiz Maker

https://www.proprofs.com/quiz-school/story.php?title=nonverbal-communication_2

Answers to Chapter 6 Exercises

Note: Though answers may vary due to experience and previous training, the following are suggested responses.

Activity 6.1: Student responses will vary as they cite a personal experience and depending on their unique use of body language communication.

Activity 6.2: Student responses will vary, but most students will probably support that a person's actions speak louder than words.

Choices 6.1: The manager's behavior is unkind and borders on being rude. One solution is simply to say, "This appears to be a bad time and I can come back later if you'd like."

NOTES:

CHAPTER 7
Written Communication

"This report, by its very length, defends itself against the risk of being read."
Winston Churchill, Former British Prime Minister

✅ SOME EXAMPLES OF WRITTEN COMMUNICATION

- Writing an e-mail message inviting 15 friends and family members to your home for a holiday get-together.

- Composing a letter to a customer about adjusting an overcharge on a recent order.

- Writing a departmental procedure outlining the steps to take when receiving and processing product returns.

 Activity 7.1 <small>Answers available at end of chapter.</small>

Business writing should be succinct—recipients should be able to access important information easily.

? Write a simple e-mail message inviting employees to the demo of a product they helped test. How will you create the message to sound concise and to the point, yet friendly?

Written Communication

The ability to write clearly and effectively when conveying a message.

 **Choices 7.1**

Older generations, including the Baby Boomers, typically do not write messages using emoticons to represent human facial expressions.

? Think about a Baby Boomer you know and imagine how he or she might react to this graphical "shorthand" of emotions so very much used and prevalent today. In other words, prior to inserting emoticons in your communications, would you take time to reflect on the reader's reactions? Why might this be important to do?

<small>Answers available at end of chapter.</small>

⚠️ KEEP THESE POINTS IN MIND ABOUT WRITTEN COMMUNICATION

- In written communication, understand ahead of time whom you are addressing and what you want your message to accomplish.

- Tone is present in all communication activities—spoken or written. The overall tone of any written message affects the reader, just as one's tone of voice in verbal exchanges affects the listener.

- Effective writing requires the ability to identify your objective and organize a series of thoughts. You then prioritize those thoughts to logically order the key points you want to make to support your objective.

- When writing an essential workplace document—such as a report or an important letter to a vendor—take time to plan it out first, then draft it, and, finally, make those critical edits and format changes to achieve the best possible final product.

- Good writers use online reference tools, including spellcheck, dictionary, and thesaurus.

- The ability to write effectively is a skill *you learn*; it comes naturally to only a few gifted individuals.

- Get to the point by presenting your primary message or call to action as quickly as possible.

- Avoid the costs of sloppy and poorly written documents containing spelling or grammatical errors—they can damage your department's or your company's reputation.

- Review and correct any formatting issues *after* the content of the document is written and edited.

 **Activity 7.2**   Answers available at end of chapter.

People long remember how a communication exchange makes them *feel*, rather than the particular words that were used. With that in mind, describe your reaction to a business letter or e-mail message you received that sounded inappropriate, rude, and/or uncaring. (**continued next page**)

EXAMPLE OF BEST PRACTICES
Written Communication
https://www.bizcoachinfo.com/archives/6493
Accessed 6/10/2018

Good business writing is vital in a number of areas, including letters, advertising copy, and presentations. Poor writing skills can hold you back or even hurt your career.

Here are some tips to help you avoid common writing errors:

- Write so your readers will understand your intended meaning.

- Eliminate unnecessary words and repetition. Remember, less is more.

- Write simply; don't use the latest buzz words or phrases.

- When writing letters or reports, start by stating your information in a condensed form, summarizing your points in an easy-to-understand way.

- If you're successful in writing a good piece, save it—especially if you think you will be preparing a similar document for another occasion.

- Proofreading their work by reading the piece out loud is one trick many writers use to avoid easy-to-miss errors.

 ## Soft Skills Tip 7.1

It doesn't matter if you organize your writing using a computer device or pen and paper—the critical thing is that you structure your thoughts clearly *before* sending off a written message, letter, e-mail, or text message.

Soft Skills Tip 7.2

Avoid using technical acronyms, jargon, and buzzwords in business correspondence and reports—especially if they will be read by readers outside your company or industry.

Activity 7.2 (continued)

Answers available at end of chapter.

? In what ways was the communiqué insensitive?

? How did the message make you *feel*?

? Did you respond in any way to the sender? Describe.

? Do you feel that written communications today are more relaxed and informal? If so, is this a good thing or a bad thing, in your opinion?

 FURTHER RESEARCH AND PRETEST LINKS

Association of Writers & Writing Programs

https://www.awpwriter.org

Pretest by ProProfs Quiz Maker

https://www.proprofs.com/quiz-school/story.php?title=test-your-writing-skills-1

Answers to Chapter 7 Exercises

Note: Though answers may vary due to experience and previous training, the following are suggested responses.

Activity 7.1: An example of a simple e-mail message inviting employees to the demo of a product they helped test is "Please join us in room 105 at 2:00 p.m. this Friday for a short demonstration of the communication software package you helped product-test recently. See you there!"

Activity 7.2: There is simply no place in the business world for inappropriate, rude, and/or uncaring verbal or written communication. Student discussion on this behavior should be lively.

Choices 7.1: Always try to be sensitive to all generations of customers—old or young. However, the guiding principle is: When in doubt, don't use emoticons.

NOTES:

PART III
Organizational & Leadership Soft Skills

Chapter 8
Project Management

Chapter 9
Creative Critical Thinking

Chapter 10
Relationship Building

Chapter 11
The Work Ethic

Part III—Organizational & Leadership Reflection Question

Think of a person you regard highly in the business world. This individual could be the CEO of a major company or a workplace manager/supervisor you have reported to.

? What are his or her greatest strengths relative to the organizational and leadership skills exhibited by this person?

? Which of the person's organizational and leadership skills could be improved, and why?

CHAPTER 8
Project Management

"Risk comes from not knowing what you're doing."
Warren Buffett, CEO, Berkshire Hathaway

✔ SOME EXAMPLES OF PROJECT MANAGEMENT

- Involving your family members in planning a fun-filled, seven-day summer vacation in Arizona, including a side trip to the Grand Canyon.

- Participating on a curriculum team to develop a new cybersecurity associate's degree at your local community college.

- Leading a team of seven employees to brainstorm an advertising plan for the launch of an upcoming product line.

 **Activity 8.1**   Answers available at end of chapter.

As a way to recognize your team's accomplishments on an important project you've just finished, you as the team leader have decided to throw a "Pizza Happy-Hour Party" at a nearby restaurant after work.

? How would you begin planning this event for next Friday evening using project management know-how? Consider these factors as you create and manage this project: the cost of the event, who will be paying for the food and drinks, which restaurant to meet at and what time, what kinds of recognition speech (if any) should be made and by whom, is it required or optional, are guests welcome, etc.

Project Management

The practice of initiating, planning, executing, controlling, and closing the work of a team to achieve specific goals and meet specific success criteria at the specified time.

 **Choices 8.1**

Project-management software is available to help coordinate activities and communications for the project team. Some organizations use this software, and some do not.

? What are the pros and cons of using automation to juggle and keep track of the project's plans, tasks, and people?

? If you had a choice as a team member, which approach would you prefer—face-to-face or software-based interactions? Explain.

Answers available at end of chapter.

⚠ KEEP THESE POINTS IN MIND ABOUT PROJECT MANAGEMENT

- A *project* is a temporary endeavor designed to produce a unique product, service, or result with a defined beginning and end. It is usually undertaken to meet unique goals and objectives or to affect a beneficial change or yield added value.

- Projects are typically broken down into phases.
  - Each phase outlines the work that needs to be completed and who is involved.
  - Generally, in order for a phase to be considered complete, specific deliverables need to be completed and handed off.

- The five project-management phases are:
  1. *Initiating*—a description of the project's product, initial documentation of project objectives, and assignment of a project manager.
  2. *Planning*—a documented project plan, and updates to the plan as the project progresses.
  3. *Executing*—verifiably completed project deliverables.
  4. *Controlling*—periodic measurement of progress, corrective action when needed, and identification of when the project is finished.
  5. *Closing*—documented acceptance of the results of the project.

- Be very clear right from the start about the roles, responsibilities, and deliverables on any project-management activity to avoid problems later.

- Be careful not to change the scope of the project as time goes by. This is called "scope creep," and it can lead to requiring more people, funds, and time than originally planned.

- Keep open and frequent communication with your team to ensure they are in the loop as the project develops.

- Take extra care to deliver the project's objectives within time and cost constraints, and to the agreed-upon quality standard.

EXAMPLE OF BEST PRACTICES
Project Management
https://thedigitalprojectmanager.com/project-management-best-practices/amp/ *Accessed 5/31/2018*

A great project-management practice is to make a point of checking in with each person on your team at least once a month. For example, if you work on a small project-management team and you're feeling ambitious, you could grab lunch with each person once a month. If you work on a large team with some members working remotely, however, this check-in could be as simple as a conversation by the coffee machine or a group video chat online.

Some questions to ask during these monthly check-ins:
- "What have you been working on lately that you are really enjoying or really disliking?"
- "How do you feel the management of this project is going, and what could be improved?"
- "Do you have the resources you need to complete the project?"

 ## Soft Skills Tip 8.1
Before starting any project, make sure it is based on a solid footing and that you have buy-in from all key stakeholders (e.g., creditors, directors, employees, government [and its agencies], owners [shareholders], suppliers).

 ## Soft Skills Tip 8.2
Being a project-management team player means asking for help when you need it. You don't want to be the person who waits too long to let others know there's a problem brewing.

 ## Activity 8.2
Answers available at end of chapter.

Your company needs to consolidate operations and relocate its headquarters and a sub-office into one location in the same city within the next six months. Time is of the essence because both current leases will expire at that time. Essentially, the major tasks will involve closing the existing headquarters and sub-office, relocating 95 employees and their office furniture to the new location, and setting up the technology infrastructure and communication design plan for the new building.

? Using the five basic project management phases presented earlier, how would you plug the aforementioned "need to do's" into the project plan? Assume that you are the team leader working with five colleagues.

FURTHER RESEARCH AND PRETEST LINKS

Project Management Institute

https://www.pmi.org/learning/library/project-management-information-system-development-5481

Pretest by ProProfs Quiz Maker

https://www.proprofs.com/quiz-school/story.php?title=project-management-fundamentals-preassessment

Answers to Chapter 8 Exercises

Note: Though answers may vary due to experience and previous training, the following are suggested responses.

Activity 8.1: Responses will vary, but ensure that each of the factors are considered and are communicated to teammates. Discussion should follow regarding: Is it a required (after-work) event? Typically, after-hours work events are not required attendance for employees.

Activity 8.2: Follow the five basic project-management phases to determine a simple and numbered approach to completing in sequence the relocation issues, technology infrastructure, and communication design plan for the new building. Responses will vary.

Choices 8.1: Automation is impersonal, but it is convenient—especially with remote team members. It is recommended to use both methods—software when appropriate, and face-to-face dialog when it is needed.

NOTES:

CHAPTER 9
Creative Critical Thinking

"Creativity is intelligence having fun."
Albert Einstein, Theoretical Physicist

SOME EXAMPLES OF CREATIVE CRITICAL THINKING

- Creating or solving a riddle.
- Writing a unique computer data analytics program for tracking customer complaints.
- Coming up with an innovative way to cut entertainment costs in your home budget.

📝 Activity 9.1 — Answers available at end of chapter.

How would you put a new spin on a company's current process of training workers? Critically reflect on these training norms:

- *Delivery Options*—online, face-to-face, or hybrid.
- *Curriculum Options*—Occupational (internships, trade schools, certificate-seeking) or college-based (degree-seeking).
- *Instructional Delivery Options*—by degreed instructors or via the Internet using TED, YouTube, videos, and the like.

? Do these norms open your mind to reflect upon and critically think about new approaches to workplace training? Briefly draft your ideas for training the next generation of workers five years from now.

Creative Critical Thinking

The ability to come up with unusual, improved, or clever ideas while analyzing information objectively to make a reasoned judgment.

Choices 9.1

Here are some examples of questions that spark critical thinking.

- What is the main point of …. ?
- What information might you need to make a decision about….?
- Do you agree that … Why or why not?
- Describe… from the perspective of …..

? How might you use these questions as prompts to help you think more creatively?

Answers available at end of chapter.

⚠ KEEP THESE POINTS IN MIND ABOUT CREATIVE CRITICAL THINKING

Critical thinking involves the evaluation of sources such as data, facts, observable phenomena, and research findings, then drawing reasonable conclusions from this information to solve a problem or make a decision. **Two examples:**

- The lead team member from the Human Resource Department analyzes the job applications submitted and decides the process by which ten applicants should be screened and selected for interviews.

- A civil attorney reviews evidence and devises a strategy to either win his client's case or decide whether or not to settle out of court.

Critical thinking often involves some level of creativity as you analyze and evaluate evidence, arguments, claims, and beliefs to first spot patterns in the information and then come up with a unique solution.

To think critically, you need to be able to put aside any assumptions or judgments and simply analyze the information you receive. As you do this, be objective and see how parts of the whole interact with each other to produce creative changes in existing systems.

You can learn to think creatively in a number of ways (e.g., experimenting, questioning assumptions, and using your imagination).

To think critically requires that you gather and evaluate information from as many different sources as possible.

Synthesize and make connections between information and arguments in order to look at situations in new ways.

Interpret information and draw conclusions to produce the best analysis you can put together.

Understand that creativity-driven innovation is a long-term, cyclical process of small successes and frequent mistakes.

Accept, analyze, and evaluate major alternative points of view.

Understand that any situation can be interpreted in different ways, so be creative and have fun!

EXAMPLE OF BEST PRACTICES
Creative Critical Thinking
https://www.forbes.com/sites/forbescoachescouncil/2018/05/31/sharpen-your-critical-thinking-skills-with-these-14-leadership-practices/amp/ *Accessed 5/31/2018*

Try any of the following practical approaches to nurture your critical-thinking skills.

- Imagine and envision what can work better, not just what has worked before.

- Reflect what you value in the organizational culture you want rather than waiting for it to arrive.

- Encourage a culture that values continuous, high-performance learning.

- Stimulate and promote the value of curiosity by conveying a "what if" openness to new ideas and situations.

 ## Activity 9.2   Answers available at end of chapter.

Recall that critical thinking helps individuals look at situations in new and different ways.

? With that in mind, what experiences have you had doing this very thing?

? Describe one or two examples of those personal or work-related experiences. Did you act on any of these creative ideas? If so, how?

Soft Skills Tip 9.1

Creativity is the act of turning new and imaginative ideas into reality. It can help individuals and teams get out of mental ruts and improve the scope and fun of their collective thinking.

 **FURTHER RESEARCH LINK**

The Foundation for Critical Thinking

http://www.criticalthinking.org/pages/critical-thinking-where-to-begin/796

Answers to Chapter 9 Exercises

Note: Though answers may vary due to experience and previous training, the following are suggested responses.

Activity 9.1: Student responses will vary about new approaches workplace training will take in five years.

Activity 9.2: Student responses will vary depending on their experiences thinking critically about problems.

Choices 9.1: Open-ended questions like these always invite diverse responses that can be creative in nature. You can then build solutions from that unique starting point.

NOTES:

CHAPTER 10
Relationship Building

> *"It is surprising how much you can accomplish if you don't care who gets the credit."*
> **Abraham Lincoln, Former U.S. President**

✅ SOME EXAMPLES OF RELATIONSHIP BUILDING

- Repeating back to someone what they said in our own words makes sure that what we heard makes sense—e.g., "What I heard you say was …".

- Recalling people's names is the first step to relationship building. Remembering other important aspects about them continues the building process.

- Sharing excitement, joy, sorrow, frustration, and disappointment helps connect us to others.

 Activity 10.1 <small>Answers available at end of chapter.</small>

People who build great relationships know…
- ◆ when to have fun and when to be serious.
- ◆ when to be over-the-top and when to be invisible.
- ◆ when to take charge and when to follow.

- **?** Describe how you have used each of these three behavioral choices in a workplace or school situation. Have your approaches served you well? Explain.

Relationship Building

Refers to the term 'relationship' as a mutual affiliation or connection between individuals or groups of people or entities; and as such, relationships are built where there is mutual understanding and caring between or among individuals.

⬆ Choices 10.1

It has been said that "a person who is appreciated will always do more than what is expected."

- **?** Do you believe this is a true statement? Why?

- **?** Can this behavior be applied easily in the workplace without necessarily increasing a person's salary or earnings? Discuss.

<small>Answers available at end of chapter.</small>

⚠ KEEP THESE POINTS IN MIND ABOUT RELATIONSHIP BUILDING

- Good relationships start with good people skills. With good working relationships, our work is more enjoyable and colleagues are more likely to support our ideas, especially ideas that are innovative or creative.

- Characteristics necessary to relationship building include:
  - *Trust*–If you trust the people you work with, you can be open and honest in your thoughts and actions, and you don't have to waste time and energy "watching your back."
  - *Mutual Respect*–When you respect the people you work with, you value their input and ideas and, in turn, they value yours.
  - *Welcoming Diversity*–People with good relationships not only accept diverse people and opinions, but, moreover, they welcome them.
  - *Keeping Commitments*—In an organization, work is interconnected. If you fail to meet deadlines and commitments, you affect the work of your co-workers. Always keep commitments; and if for some reason you cannot, make sure all affected individuals know what happened.

- Step up to help someone before you are asked—especially if you see a colleague struggling.

- Take a little time every day to do something nice for someone you know—not because you are expected to, but simply because you can.

- Take responsibility and apologize when you have acted poorly. We all behave badly from time to time, and we have the power to fix that behavior in positive ways.

EXAMPLE OF BEST PRACTICES
Relationship Building
https://www.mindtools.com/pages/article/newCDV_85.htm
Accessed 6/8/2018

Like it or loathe it, office politics are a fact of life in any organization and can get in the way of good and trusting relationship building. Your first instinct may be to keep your distance from people who practice "bad" politics. In fact, the opposite can be more effective. The expression "Keep your friends close and your enemies closer" often applies to office politics.

So, get to know the gossips and manipulators within your organization better. Be courteous but guarded, as they may repeat what you say with a negative "spin." Try to understand their goals so you can avoid or counter the impact of their negative politicking. And be aware that some people behave badly because they feel insecure.

 ## Activity 10.2   Answers available at end of chapter.

The opportunity to observe in another department periodically allows employees to participate in relationship building that enhances cross-department cooperation and understanding. It also offers employees a chance to become aware of and explore other career paths.

?   In what ways does this opportunity help not only the worker, but the organization as well?

 ## Soft Skills Tip 10.1

Workplace power struggles are, at times, at the root of office politics. Many people approach this type of conflict with a "win-lose" attitude. Such an attitude tends to destroy the organizational culture. Best advice: *Don't get involved.*

Soft Skills Tip 10.2

Take the time and expend the energy to thank, reward, and recognize the contributions of people who help you look good and succeed.

 **FURTHER RESEARCH LINK**

The Challenge of Workplace Relationships

https://capitaleap.org/blog/2013/06/12/workplace-relationships-navigating-the-choppy-waters-of-the-work-place/

Answers to Chapter 10 Exercises

Note: Though answers may vary due to experience and previous training, the following are suggested responses.

Activity 10.1: Responses will vary depending on students' unique experiences in relationship building—considering the type of work, setting for the interaction, familiarization with workplace communicators, and other variables.

Activity 10.2: Encouraging interdepartmental switch days is a great activity within organizations—promoting workplace friendships based on respect and common behaviors. One of the biggest benefits is that it is a wonderful training ground for cross-training, personal growth and better worker morale.

Choices 10.1: The statement has merit. Whether in our personal or work lives, being appreciated and recognized is often regarded as being worth more than money to many persons.

NOTES:

CHAPTER 11

The Work Ethic

"I never left the field saying I could have done more to get ready, and that gives me peace of mind."
Peyton Manning, Football Quarterback

✓ SOME EXAMPLES OF THE WORK ETHIC

- Working 10 minutes past quitting time without being asked, just to carefully proofread a company document one last time.

- Preparing a simple procedures manual describing the key activities of your current job so the person replacing you in the job next month will be informed.

- Demonstrating "grace under pressure" will show your boss that your work ethic is strong enough for a future job promotion or pay raise.

 Activity 11.1 Answers available at end of chapter.

Some people in the United States believe that "a person's work ethic is grounded in the idea that a person should do his or her share to contribute to the economic survival of society through working."

? Do you agree with this statement about a person's work ethic? Why or why not?

? Present this same statement to three other people you know (friends, family, or classmates) and record their responses. Be prepared to discuss your discoveries as a result of this activity in class.

The Work Ethic

A set of moral principles an employee uses in his job based on a belief in the benefit and importance of work and its inherent ability to strengthen character.

 ## Soft Skills Tip 11.1

Organizations need workers who are self-disciplined and have a good work ethic because those employees will push themselves to complete work tasks without needing others to intervene and help them out at the last minute.

⚠ KEEP THESE POINTS IN MIND ABOUT THE WORK ETHIC

- Having a strong work ethic isn't the same thing as being a workaholic. It is a way of describing a number of qualities that, together, create value in an employee.

- A positive attitude will affect many aspects of your work. Top among these is, it will help you cope with pressure and stress as well as allow you to be more flexible in your job.

- Employees with a good work ethic consistently exhibit the following behaviors:
  - ◆ *Integrity* fosters trusting relationships with clients, co-workers, and team leaders.
  - ◆ *Sense of responsibility* shows when employees get to work on time, put in their best effort, and complete projects to the best of their ability.
  - ◆ *Being dependable* means they will do what they say they are going to do, such as being on time to meetings and completing projects on schedule.

- Improve your attitude and succeed at work by spending time with people who have a positive attitude and avoiding those who are negative and who complain frequently.

- When discussing a project with a co-worker, seek to analyze problems without assigning blame—the focus is on solving them.

- Follow through with commitments you make, and do so in a reliable and dependable way.

- Be among the first to forgive others when they come up short. It happens to each of us from time to time.

- While at work, check your e-mail only two or three times a day. Turn off notifications and leave social media for after work.

✐ Activity 11.2

Answers available at end of chapter.

Describe the work ethic of two people you know; for example, a family member, teacher, or boss. One person has a great work ethic in your opinion, and the other person simply does not.

? How would you compare your two descriptions?

? In particular, which work ethic factors do you admire, and which ones do you find inadequate according to your personal work ethic?

EXAMPLE OF BEST PRACTICES
The Work Ethic
https://www.thebalancecareers.com/best-ways-you-can-show-strong-work-ethic-4157720
Accessed 7/28/2018

What Does a Strong Work Ethic Look Like?

Since you can't peer into another employee's soul, you have to judge their work ethic based on their output. So, what does a strong work ethic look like? A person who displays a strong work ethic takes these actions:

- *Shows up on time, every day.* This doesn't necessarily mean that you need to work a 9:00 to 5:00 job. But when you are supposed to be at work, you are at work.

- *Does what needs to be done.* A person with a strong work ethic will tackle the icky tasks as well as the interesting ones. It may not be "your" job, but if it needs to get done, you will make sure that it gets done.

- *Doesn't whine.* Work is hard. That's why it is called work. But, just because something is hard, doesn't mean that you have to complain about it. Just do it.

- *Works through bad situations.* A person with a strong work ethic doesn't call in sick because of a cold, or bad weather. Now, on occasion, a person with a strong work ethic should call in sick and doesn't. While this may seem noble, it's not. Sharing your germs or driving under unsafe conditions doesn't make you a superstar, it makes you dangerous. Don't encourage this bad side of a strong work ethic.

- *Gets the job done.* A good work ethic means nothing if you can't deliver the expected finished product at the end.

 # Choices 11.1

Your company urges employees to work in teams. Brent is a co-worker with whom you have worked before—and in your opinion, he has repeatedly displayed a poor attitude. That is to say, it appears that he is often angry and intentionally seems to put others down through joking without realizing his words may be hurtful and insulting. In addition, he rarely completes assigned projects on time, leaving others to cover for him. Most co-workers simply try to have little to do with him.

? As a co-worker, what would be your approach with Brent given his work ethic?

? As Brent's supervisor, what action would you take?

? Describe the behavior of other people you've worked with that are similar to Brent's.

Answers available at end of chapter.

FURTHER RESEARCH AND PRETEST LINKS

Kauffman Entrepreneurs: Eight Elements of an Ethical Organization
https://www.entrepreneurship.org/articles/2002/12/eight-elements-of-an-ethical-organization

Pretest by ProProfs Quiz Maker: Work Ethic Vocabulary Words
https://www.proprofs.com/quiz-school/story.php?title=work-ethic-vocabulary-words

Answers to Chapter 11 Exercises

Note: Though answers may vary due to experience and previous training, the following are suggested responses.

Activity 11.1: Student responses will vary and most likely will be influenced by personal experiences and their formed opinions.

Activity 11.2: Though student responses will differ, they should mention the importance of integrity, a sense of responsibility, and dependability.

Choices 11.1: In general, workers avoid co-workers like Brent because of his behavior. Perhaps he is insecure and needs a friend to be better accepted by co-workers. Brent needs to be told how his behavior is affecting his colleagues and the general work environment and productivity.

NOTES:

PART IV
Interpersonal Soft Skills

Chapter 12
Problem Solving

Chapter 13
Team Building/Teamwork

Chapter 14
Negotiation

Chapter 15
Collaboration

Part IV—Interpersonal Reflection Question

Describe a time (personal- or workplace-oriented) when you were part of a team effort and really enjoyed the experience.

? With that situation in mind, what made the experience fun and worthwhile?

? Identify a time in your work experience where you used your skills as a negotiator. Upon reflection, would you rate yourself successful in this situation? Why, or why not?

CHAPTER 12
Problem Solving

*"Every problem is a gift.
Without them, we wouldn't grow."*
Tony Robbins, Author and Life Coach

✔ SOME EXAMPLES OF PROBLEM SOLVING

- Deciding which rental home will best fit your budget and the needs of your family of four.

- Determining the best approach for reducing theft of merchandise at a family-run retail store.

- Selecting the best examples to use when training employees how to create and manipulate Excel's pivot tables.

 Activity 12.1 Answers available at end of chapter.

When brainstorming, remember to...
- concentrate on the problem at hand.
- entertain all ideas openly.
- refrain from allowing members to evaluate others' ideas on the spot.

Issue to Brainstorm: The CEO has told hourly employees that the current overtime policy will be changed to cut overtime pay hours by 50 percent. Currently the policy states: "Overtime pay is funded up to 10 hours a week."

(continued on Page 55)

Problem Solving
The process of working through the details of a problem to reach a solution.

 **Choices 12.1**

When deciding a course of action, consider either:
- *Reasoning*—using the facts and figures to make decisions, or
- *Intuition*—using your 'gut feeling' about possible courses of action to take.

Though intuition is an acceptable means of decision making, it is generally more appropriate when the decision is simple or needs to be made quickly.

? For the most part, how do you make decisions—using your intuition or by reasoning?

? What influences you when determining which approach to use? Discuss.

Answers available at end of chapter.

⚠ KEEP THESE POINTS IN MIND ABOUT PROBLEM SOLVING

- Decision making and problem solving are ongoing processes of evaluating situations or problems. In large part, these processes depend on the *right* information being available to the *right* people at the *right* times.

- The problem-solving process consists of the following five steps:

    1. *Identify and define the problem.* You must try to solve the *right* problem and not get sidetracked with the symptoms. Identify the problem by asking the right questions and learning from the responses.

    2. *Analyze the problem and causes.* How often does the problem occur? How severe is it? What might be the causes of the problem? How long has it been going on? Has it gotten worse?

    3. *Identify decision criteria.* How will you weigh the criteria? What will the decision be based on?

    4. *Develop alternative solutions.* Do not stop at the first solution you identify. Evaluate other viable scenarios and assess the pros and cons of each.

    5. *Choose and implement the optimal solution.* Develop a base of support that will ensure you can apply the solution. Prepare for contingencies as well.

- Define accurately the problem at hand, because it affects all the steps that follow. If the problem is inaccurately defined, every step in the decision-making process will be based on an incorrect starting point.

- One of the best-known methods for developing alternatives is through brainstorming, where a group tasked with the problem works together to generate ideas. The assumption behind brainstorming is that the group dynamic stimulates thinking. In other words, one person's ideas, no matter how outrageous, can generate ideas from other group members. Ideally, this spawning of ideas is contagious; and before long, lots of suggestions and ideas flow. Brainstorming usually requires 30 minutes to an hour to complete.

- Solve problems systematically by taking these steps:
    - Place the problem in context
    - Do not jump to conclusions
    - Evaluate alternatives
    - Follow through with a contingency plan, should it be needed

EXAMPLE OF BEST PRACTICES
Problem Solving

http://www.growthresource.com/best-practices/best-practice-problem-solving.html *Accessed 5/30/2018*

Getting the Right People on the Right Problems

As you compose a team to tackle a particular problem, it's important to select candidates carefully. You need three types of people on any team problem-solving effort.

- *Deciders* hold the authority and are the "bosses."
- *Doers* are implementers who will get the job done.
- *Experts* bring knowledge and expertise to the table.

 ## Activity 12.2 Answers available at end of chapter.

As stated in the Best Practices feature above, three types of people are needed when problem solving: Deciders, Doers, and Experts.

? Which of the three roles do you think your co-workers would say is your strongest when solving problems?

? Why might they identify that particular role for you? Explain.

Activity 12.1 (continued) Answers at end of chapter.

Your objective is to recommend a second alternative for the CEO to consider. To come up with this recommendation, you will brainstorm an optional solution with a team of five co-workers.

? Who should be on the overtime pay team?

? What steps should the team take to brainstorm a new or altered policy?

? Why do you think the CEO should consider the merits of the team's suggestions?

 ## Soft Skills Tip 12.1

Companies look for and need problem-solvers who can gracefully navigate unexpected challenges and come up with effective and workable solutions to problems.

📖 FURTHER RESEARCH AND PRETEST LINKS

Free Management Library: Problem Solving and Decision Making
https://managementhelp.org/personalproductivity/problem-solving.htm

Pretest by Quizizz: Problem Solving
https://quizizz.com/admin/quiz/57f691aef70e1da63b50b7b4

Answers to Chapter 12 Exercises

Note: Though answers may vary due to experience and previous training, the following are suggested responses.

Activity 12.1: Brainstorming is fun, especially when it comes to suggesting pay issues to upper management. The CEO made a good decision to ask for input from the staff before making a final policy decision on pay. In general, the overtime pay team should be representative of workers who typically work overtime. The brainstorming process covered in the chapter should be followed. As a result of having been asked, it is likely that there will be more buy-in from workers once the new policy is in place.

Activity 12.2: Student responses will vary.

Choices 12.1: When problem solving, people with experience in the issue will respond with a "gut-felt" approach when finding an acceptable resolution to the problem. It depends on the nature of the problem, in most cases, as to which approach is best to use.

NOTES:

CHAPTER 13
Team Building/Teamwork

"Talent wins games, but teamwork and intelligence win championships."
Michael Jordan, American Basketball Player

✓ SOME EXAMPLES OF TEAM BUILDING/TEAMWORK

- Playing on a volleyball team offered through your city's recreation department.

- Serving on your company's benefits package review team to bring health benefits more in line with changing health-care needs and costs.

- Volunteering to serve on a planning committee to determine next year's professional development training activities.

✎ Activity 13.1   Answers available at end of chapter.

Assume you were assigned to a team at work dealing with a project area under your expertise. However, among the four other persons assigned to the team, you have had work-related disagreements or minor heated discussions with two of them over the past six months.

? How would you successfully serve on this team given those situations? Consider:
   ◆ You have no choice about serving as you've been assigned to do so by your manager.
   ◆ You know you have to start out on the "right foot" with these particular teammates.

? How would you proceed to repair past issues with these individuals?

Team Building/Teamwork
The action or process whereby a group of people work together effectively as a cohesive team, in order to accomplish activities or agreed-upon goals.

💡 Soft Skills Tip 13.1
To maintain good working relationships, any negative feedback you offer a co-worker should be focused on a specific task, not on his or her personality. To be constructive, any criticism you offer should be accompanied by a positive suggestion on how to improve the task.

⚠ KEEP THESE POINTS IN MIND ABOUT TEAM BUILDING/TEAMWORK

- The new structural workplace model—"network of teams"—is one in which companies build and empower teams to work on specific business projects and challenges.

- Interconnected and flexible teams are one reason companies around the world are becoming more agile and customer-focused. These teams are defined by a high degree of empowerment, strong communication links, and swift information flow among members.

- Empowered teams set their own goals and make their own decisions within the context of a central strategy or business plan.

- Teambuilding moves workers into customer-, product-, or market-focused groups that are led by team leaders, *not* "professional functional managers."

- A team's characteristics include being on-demand, as needed, with people coming together to tackle projects. They then disband and move on to other individual or team projects.

- It is important to develop common goals so that all team members understand how their efforts are feeding into the larger objectives and/or plan.

- While completing any task, try hard to stick to deadlines you are assigned so colleagues can depend on and trust that you will do team-assigned tasks in a timely manner.

- Always act with integrity by sharing project information fully with team members to achieve desired results.

- For a change, hold team meetings out of the office occasionally to remove everyday distractions and busyness.

📝 Activity 13.2

Answers available at end of chapter.

During a weekly team meeting, you notice that one of your co-workers is more quiet than usual. David acts as if he does not care to be involved in the team's weekly gatherings. Respond to the following three statements indicating what you might say to David, who appears to be suffering from a lack of motivation.

- **?** You *acknowledge* David's value by saying….
- **?** You *discover* the source of the problem by asking….
- **?** You *stress* the importance of team harmony by suggesting….

EXAMPLE OF BEST PRACTICES
Team Building/Teamwork
http://fortune.com/2016/06/27/team-building-leaders-whitepages/ *Accessed 6/12/2018*

How do you build a strong team?
by Alex Algard, CEO of Whitepages

"A strong team is one of the single best indicators of a company's long-term success. And finding and hiring the right people is one of the hardest challenges any manager will encounter over the course of their careers. In my early days of hiring at Whitepages, my first instinct was to focus too much on fluffy resume bullet points, flashy company names, and prestigious schools. While these things can be predictive of success, they often misrepresent the true quality of a candidate.

"What I have found over time is that a good rule to live by is to not put too much emphasis on whether candidates fit a job description. Instead, determine whether they are the kind of people you want to work closely with—day in and day out.

"The strongest players on every team I've built all had the following core character traits: versatility, self-motivation, passion, and conviction."

 # Choices 13.1

As mentioned in the *Keep These Points in Mind* feature, workers are increasingly operating as a *network of teams* alongside traditional structures, with people moving from team to team rather than remaining in static, more formal arrangements. Most times, when that occurs, it creates a *synergy* that produces a collective effort greater than the sum of their individual efforts.

? In your experience, does synergy really work within groups? Explain and cite a *synergy example* from a personal or work experience.

Answers available at end of chapter.

 **FURTHER RESEARCH AND PRETEST LINKS**

Free Management Library: All About Team Building

https://managementhelp.org/groups/team-building.htm

Top Personality Tests for Teambuilding

https://www.2ecreative.com/top-personality-tests-for-team-building/

Answers to Chapter 13 Exercises

Note: Though answers may vary due to experience and previous training, the following are suggested responses.

Activity 13.1: It is critical to begin any project management activity with all outstanding issues among the participants completely cleared up. This situation should shout "honest and clear communication" among team members or the success of the team will quickly go downhill.

Activity 13.2: David needs some one-on-one time with a co-worker who provides sincere encouragement and acknowledges the genuine and keen contributions he makes to the team.

Choices 13.1: Yes, *synergy* is effective when groups, teams, or organizations work collectively. Ideas spinning off many people at one time is fun and allows relationships to build and organizations to thrive and become more successful.

NOTES:

CHAPTER 14
Negotiation

"We cannot negotiate with people who say what's mine is mine and what's yours is negotiable."
John F. Kennedy, Former U.S. President

✔ SOME EXAMPLES OF NEGOTIATION

- Determining with a locally hired handyman the fair cost of fixing four items in your condo.

- Figuring out with your boss how to temporarily reduce in-office work hours due to a sudden family health emergency.

- Re-evaluating with your manager the additional workload recently assigned you, given that you feel your current tasks occupy almost all of your time as it is.

 Activity 14.1 Answers available at end of chapter.

As a service rep, you are in a discussion with an unhappy customer who is pushing you to accept all her terms in order to keep her as a customer. But you are feeling that the customer is pushing you into a corner and you do not agree with her resolution. You feel that it is okay to say "no" when that's the right answer.

? By using effective negotiation skills in this encounter, how might you respectfully respond to the customer, thereby putting less revenue at risk and keeping more customers in the process?

Negotiation

An interpersonal process by which people settle differences and conflicts by compromise or agreement in an effort to avoid argument and dispute—a kind of give-and-take approach between the participants.

 **Choices 14.1**

It has been said that during the negotiation process, you should be willing to walk away. In other words, never negotiate without options.

? Think about the last time you walked away from a conflict—personal or business related. In retrospect, was it the right thing to do at the time? Discuss.

? Would you take that same action today? Discuss.

Answers available at end of chapter.

⚠ KEEP THESE POINTS IN MIND ABOUT NEGOTIATION

- In any negotiation, individuals understandably aim to achieve the best possible outcome for their position or the organization they represent. However, applying the principles of fairness, seeking mutual benefit, and maintaining a relationship are keys to any successful outcome.

- The negotiation process encompasses six steps:
  1. *Preparing to Meet*—Before any negotiation takes place, a decision needs to be made as to when and where a meeting will take place and who will be invited to attend.
  2. *Discussing the Issues*—During this stage, individuals or members of each side put forward the case as they see it (i.e., their understanding of the situation). Each side should have an equal opportunity and timeframe to fully present its case.
  3. *Clarifying Goals*—The goals, interests, and viewpoints of both sides need to be clarified. It is helpful to list these factors in order of priority.
  4. *Negotiating Toward a Win-Win Outcome*—This stage focuses on what is termed a 'win-win' outcome where both sides feel they have gained something positive through the process of negotiation, and both sides feel their points of view have been taken into consideration.
  5. *Gaining Agreement*—Agreement can be achieved once understanding of both sides' viewpoints and interests are considered.
  6. *Implementing a Course of Action*—Stemming from the agreement, a course of action must be implemented to carry through the decision.

- Conflict resolution requires some degree of negotiation, because if conflicts are allowed to fester and grow, the disagreements will ultimately diminish organizational productivity and damage staff morale.

- Employers value employees with the skills to manage and diffuse conflicts.

- Avoid taking the discussion issues or the other person's behavior personally during the negotiation.

- During negotiations, focus on solving the problem, which is: How can we conclude an agreement that respects the needs of *both* parties?

- Make accurate decisions by understanding the other side's situation. The more information you have, the stronger negotiator you will be.

Negotiation

EXAMPLE OF BEST PRACTICES

Negotiation

https://startupnation.com/manage-your-business/
10-techniques-for-better-negotiation/
Accessed 5/30/2018

Here are some tactics to become a more confident negotiator:

- Prepare, prepare, prepare. Make sure you are clear on what you really want out of the negotiated deal.

- Leave behind your ego. The best negotiators either don't care or don't *show* they care about who gets credit for a successful deal.

- Ramp up your listening skills. The best negotiators are often quiet listeners who patiently let others have the floor while they make their case. They never interrupt.

- Anticipate compromise. You should expect to make concessions and plan what they might be. Stick to your principles, though. If you find negotiations crossing those boundaries, it might be a deal you can live without.

- Close with confirmation. At the close of any meeting (even if no final deal is struck), recap the points covered and any areas of agreement. Make sure everyone confirms these closing points.

 # Soft Skills Tip 14.1

You can become an effective negotiator by allowing the other person to do most of the talking. For example, follow the *70/30 Rule*—listen 70 percent of the time and talk only 30 percent of the time.

Encourage the other negotiator to talk by asking lots of *open-ended questions*—meaning, questions that cannot be answered with a simple "yes" or "no." For example, pose questions that begin with *Who, What, How, Why, When,* and *Where* to encourage more open discussion and understanding of the underlying issues causing concern.

 **Activity 14.2**

Answers available at end of chapter.

Assume you are at a job interview for a software programmer position. You are about to be hired, but the interviewer has one last question to clear up—your starting salary. Your task—negotiate your way from a salary of $50K to $55K. You offer the following: a) you were second top graduate in the software programming associate's degree program at the local community college, and b) you have previous experience through coding miscellaneous programming jobs for your uncle at his mid-size local office supply business over the past six years.

? At this point in your interview, how would you proceed?

? Typically, would you prepare yourself for this interview question ahead of time? Explain.

 **FURTHER RESEARCH LINK**

Ethical Systems: Negotiation

http://www.ethicalsystems.org/content/negotiation

Answers to Chapter 14 Exercises

Note: Though answers may vary due to experience and previous training, the following are suggested responses.

Activity 14.1: It is possible that some students will respond that you should never argue with a customer. However, others might suggest that the service rep might respond by saying: "We see this differently, and I am going to have to put more thought to the perspective you have shared with me. It's helpful for me to understand how you see things, and I thank you for that. In the meantime, here is what I can do to solve the immediate problem."

Activity 14.2: When it comes to negotiating a starting salary at a company, stress your experience and the value you bring to the job. If appropriate, mention your past pay history from similar employment.

Choices 14.1: We all learn from the actions we take—good and bad. Most student responses will support the willingness to walk away from negotiations, if needed.

NOTES:

CHAPTER 15
Collaboration

"Many ideas grow better when transplanted into another mind than the one where they sprang up."
Oliver Wendell Holmes,
Former U.S. Supreme Court Justice

✓ SOME EXAMPLES OF COLLABORATION

- Analyzing problematic issues with team members surrounding an ongoing project without assigning blame.

- Shadowing a team member during work hours to understand better the complexities of the other person's role and responsibilities.

- Sharing your feelings and job-related frustrations with your company's Human Resource Director.

✎ Activity 15.1 Answers available at end of chapter.

Most everyone likes it when victories are shared—that's one of the most positive outcomes when collaborating with others. However, Keanna, a fellow teammate, is noticeably upset at work this morning. Yesterday, work was incredibly difficult for her because the team meeting took *forever* and her ideas went unacknowledged. She really felt down by the end of the day!

Today, Keanna confided in you that, after talking with her husband last night, she is thinking about **(continued next page)**

Collaboration

The process of working with others to create or produce a deliverable organizational goal.

⋔ Choices 15.1

Carson feels that he is good at collaborating with others because he is flexible and willing to make necessary compromises to achieve his group's stated goal. But lately, Carson feels he is being pushed too hard by teammates to agree on issues. He is becoming more angry at each weekly team meeting.

? Should Carson just stay quiet and seethe, or should he speak up and get his feelings and irritations out in the open?

? What factors might cause either approach to work? Discuss.

Answers available at end of chapter.

⚠ KEEP THESE POINTS IN MIND ABOUT COLLABORATION

- Sometimes collaboration is defined simply as teamwork taken to a higher level.

- Collectively put the desired project results at the *forefront*—this isn't about the individual goals of one or two people on the team.

- When collaborating, you must be willing as a teammate to apologize for missteps and forgive others for mistakes.

- As you collaborate, try switching most remote communication to regular video calls, which are a much better vehicle for establishing rapport and creating empathy than either e-mails or voice calls.

- The benefits of collaboration include the following:
  - *It encourages open communication* among all team members, who share information necessary to carry out tasks.
  - *It builds consensus or agreement* about goals and methods for completing projects or tasks.
  - *It identifies obstacles and problems* as they occur. As a group, team members plug each other's gaps and grow beyond their comfort zones as they more easily take risks collectively.
  - *It accelerates action.* A problem that could take months to get resolved when handled by a single individual may take just a few hours to resolve when several other members contribute their unique standpoints, approaches, and expertise.

Activity 15.1 (continued)
<small>Answers available at end of chapter.</small>

quitting her job. You are aware that she has other things going on in her life—most notably, her aging father, who, now in the beginning stages of Alzheimer's disease, has recently moved in with Keanna, her husband, and their two teenage children.

? If you were having a private conversation with Keanna, what would you say to calm her down so that she can approach the situation more rationally? You and others know she contributes significantly each time her team collaborates on issues.

? What do you think is really behind Keanna's wanting to quit her job at this point in time?

Collaboration

EXAMPLE OF BEST PRACTICES
Collaboration

https://hbr.org/sponsored/2018/02/how-disney-creates -a-culture-of-collaboration-and-constructive-conflict   *Accessed 7/23/2018*

Collaboration itself is not always easy to achieve, but it's a critical step toward cultivating something that can be even more beneficial. This is where ideas like challenging the status quo start to become so important, and it's why we define constructive conflict as conflict that is clearly focused on moving teams and the organization forward. It can happen only in a trusting and risk-tolerant environment that leaders must intentionally establish, operationalize, and sustain over time.

So, how can leaders enable this type of culture within their organization? To start, they can work to foster an environment where team members feel comfortable doing three things:

- Conveying and expressing their ideas with leadership *and with each other* in a way that is clearly understood.

- *Listening carefully and intentionally* when other team members are speaking.

- Engaging in open and passionate debate *of ideas and opinions*.

 ## Soft Skills Tip 15.1

Collaboration and modern technologies are allowing teams to have access to the same information from any place in the world, as video conferencing paired with instant messaging typically decreases the time relegated to meetings and minimizes pricey business trips.

 ## Soft Skills Tip 15.2

Collaboration requires teams to assume *shared responsibility* for the work product and to value the individual contributions of each team member.

 # Activity 15.2

Answers available at end of chapter.

Marjorie Jacks has just taken a new management position at Maricopa Marketing Enterprises and is starting to realize how difficult it is to bring together individuals who have varying skills, contrasting personalities, and different responsibilities. At a recent professional marketing conference she attended, she heard a presentation on teambuilding that she may implement. It involves team members donating their time and/or money to charitable causes. **(continued next page)**

Activity 15.2 (continued)

Answers available at end of chapter.

The program allows team members two to three work days each year where they can go and donate their time to a charitable cause. The employees are encouraged to go in groups and help out together. Some examples include mentoring at nearby schools, building houses for veterans, and volunteering at homeless shelters to provide meals and job training.

? What are some pros and cons of this approach to build collaboration?

? Do you personally think this approach is viable and would build a greater collaborative workplace? Why?

FURTHER RESEARCH AND PRETEST LINKS

Grantmakers for Effective Organizations (Collaboration)
https://www.geofunders.org/what-we-care-about/collaboration

Pretest by ProProfs Quiz Maker
https://www.proprofs.com/quiz-school/story.php?title=collaboration

Answers to Chapter 15 Exercises

Note: Though answers may vary due to experience and previous training, the following are suggested responses.

Activity 15.1: Sometimes it is difficult for personal circumstances not to affect performance on the job. This scenario with Keanna is a prime example. Most companies will provide workers with assistance when dealing with personal issues. The key action to take now is to listen to Keanna and suggest she speak to her manager or the Human Resource Department.

Activity 15.2: Student responses will vary, but credit should be given to Marjorie Jacks' efforts to improve collaborative activities within the organization.

Choices 15.1: It sounds like Carson needs involved assistance by a close team member or the team leader. It would help everyone if Carson would speak up and share how he is feeling, though.

NOTES:

PART V
Self-Management Soft Skills

Chapter 16
Time Management

Chapter 17
Stress Management

Chapter 18
Professional Awareness

Part V—Self-Management Reflection Question

Reflect on your strongest self-management skill. Is it time management, or is it stress management?

? What actions do you intentionally take to manage your time well?

? What actions do you intentionally take to manage your stress within reason?

Time Management

> *"Time has no meaning in itself unless we choose to give it significance."*
> Leo Buscaglia, Author & Motivational Speaker

✅ SOME EXAMPLES OF TIME MANAGEMENT

- Scheduling a recently assigned priority project into an already busy day.

- Creating a *to-do list*, then prioritizing the tasks listed based on their organizational importance.

- Keeping a neat and organized work area, desk, and office-supply closet is a must when managing your time. Valuable time is lost searching through clutter or stacks of paper for a specific item that you need at a moment's notice.

📝 Activity 16.1 — Answers available at end of chapter.

? Provide an example of how you have implemented or would apply each time-management task below:

- ◆ Complete deadline work early

- ◆ Stay organized

- ◆ Deal skillfully with interruptions by co-workers

Time Management

The ability to use one's time effectively, efficiently and productively.

✝ Choices 16.1

His co-workers affectionately call him "last-minute Sam." Sam has a good heart and means well, but he always completes his projects at the very last minute, causing stress to himself and others. Some colleagues, however, don't let Sam's work patterns bother them.

? What would your reaction be if Sam were a colleague of yours?

? Would you allow his behavior to affect you?

Answers available at end of chapter.

⚠ KEEP THESE POINTS IN MIND ABOUT TIME MANAGEMENT

- Employees who manage their time well are more productive, more efficient, and more likely to meet deadlines because they know where they are going and how to get there. Why? They simply and consistently *make a plan* to do it.

- When analyzing workload, focus on the most important and time-sensitive tasks, and limit the amount of time wasted on non-essential duties. Assign priorities and maintain focus on what needs to be completed.

- To manage your time effectively, you should learn and apply these skills:
  - Before prioritizing tasks, set short- and long-term goals—making certain every task on your to-do list contributes to at least one goal.
  - Keep your focus on completing daily tasks and getting closer to your goals.
  - Don't allow instant messaging, social media, and distractions from phones and meetings to take up your time while working toward goals.
  - When assigning priorities, consider such factors as when each task needs to be done, how long it might take, and how important it might be to others in the organization. Once this information has been gathered, plan and prioritize accordingly.

- Work on more complex and high-priority tasks when you have the highest energy and sharpest concentration.

- Break projects up into manageable parts so you don't feel overwhelmed. Crossing smaller tasks off your list lets you know that you are making progress toward completing the job.

- Avoid being a perfectionist—instead, set realistic standards for quality and do your best to meet the goals and the standards you have set.

- Don't permit others to manage your time for you.

EXAMPLE OF BEST PRACTICES
Time Management
https://www.startups.co/articles/how-fortune-500-leaders-schedule-their-days *Accessed 6/10/2018*

Some of the best, brightest, and most successful leaders' daily routines are structured starting from the moment their feet touch the floor in the morning, to the moment their head hits the pillow at night. While everyone has a different routine that works for them, it's important to formulate and sustain habits that will improve your work/life balance, professional focus, and personal development. The following are all examples from the daily routines of Fortune 500 leaders, which you can learn from and replicate in your daily schedule to achieve greater success both at work and at home.

- Apple CEO Tim Cook starts each day sending and responding to emails at 4:30 a.m.

- John Mackey, founder of Whole Foods, starts his day with a nutrient-rich breakfast smoothie.

- Ken Chenault, CEO of American Express, writes down three things before leaving the office that he wants to accomplish the next day.

 ## Activity 16.2 Answers available at end of chapter.

"To-Do List" Questions:

? What are the pros and cons of using a *continuous* to-do list created on a yellow pad versus making a *new* to-do list *each* day—for example, on a 3"x5" index card?

? Which approach fits you best? Explain reasons for your choice.

 # Soft Skills Tip 16.1

Time management isn't about doing more tasks—it's about doing the *right* tasks on time or when you've made a promise to do so. To-do lists, properly prioritized and integrated with your schedule, are a great way to avoid forgetting to do something and speak to your professionalism.

 # Soft Skills Tip 16.2

It is inevitable that some tasks will be interrupted or delayed partway through completion. Making a commitment to return to the task helps you limit the number of tasks you are working on at a given time.

 **FURTHER RESEARCH AND PRETEST LINKS**

Life Hack: Top 15 Time Management Apps and Tools
https://www.lifehack.org/articles/technology/top-15-time-management-apps-and-tools.html

Pretest Activa Training: 4-Minute Time Management Test
https://www.activia.co.uk/time-management-test

Answers to Chapter 16 Exercises

Note: Though answers may vary due to experience and previous training, the following are suggested responses.

Activity 16.1: Student responses will vary.

Activity 16.2: Student responses will vary. However, the key point here is not *what* you use to keep on top of tasks, but that you use some means to help you schedule that results in being able to manage your time better.

Choices 16.1: It is important to try to work with Sam; but if he chooses not to manage his time better, it is better not to rely on him to be part of working on your future projects.

NOTES:

CHAPTER 17
Stress Management

"Our anxiety does not come from thinking about the future, but from wanting to control it."
Khalil Gibran, Writer and Poet

✓ SOME EXAMPLES OF STRESS MANAGEMENT

- Accepting help from supportive family and friends improves your ability to manage stress and change unhealthy behaviors.

- Identifying the events or situations that *trigger your stressful feelings*. These may be related to your children, family, financial decisions, health, or work relationships.

- Practicing relaxation techniques such as meditation, yoga, or tai-chi.

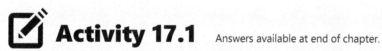 **Activity 17.1** Answers available at end of chapter.

Stress is bad—or is it? Interestingly, researchers have found evidence suggesting that some stress is actually good because it can help us cope better with life's events. These simple stress management activities are designed to curb your worries:

- Jot it down—transferring stressful thoughts from your head onto paper can help.
- Move your body—release endorphins that make you feel less stressed and more positive.
(continued next page)

Stress Management
A wide spectrum of techniques aimed at controlling a person's level of stress.

 **Choices 17.1**

Should you ask your boss for a raise? Most workers know that meetings of this type can manifest into stomach-clenching stress. Here are some approaches to reduce it:

- Get confident by listing all your accomplishments from the past year.
- Rehearse what you will say.
- Talk about why your work deserves better compensation.
- If your boss says no, ask how you can work toward a raise or promotion over the coming six months so you'll be more prepared at your next meeting.

Answers available at end of chapter.

⚠ KEEP THESE POINTS IN MIND ABOUT STRESS MANAGEMENT

● Stress is an automatic physical, mental, and emotional response to a challenging event, and a normal part of everyone's life. When channeled positively, stress can lead to growth, action, and change. Negative stress, however, can lessen your quality of life.

● Many events can trigger the stress reaction, including danger, threat, news, illness, or significant changes in one's life like the death of a loved one, a separation or divorce, or losing a job.

● We can never eliminate stress from our lives; stressful situations are simply part of everybody's day. Nonetheless, we can learn to react to stress in a positive manner and take control of the situation rather than allowing the stress to remain in control.

● Positive stress can motivate and energize a person; negative stress often makes a person feel anxious and frustrated.

● Get rid of unwanted stress by trying these suggestions:
  ◆ Stop getting mentally and emotionally strained if you are unhappy in your job, relationship, or parenting—instead, act to change your situation.
  ◆ Make plans to complete an unfinished task or decide to drop it altogether and stop causing yourself stress over it.
  ◆ Recognize that you worry about things you can do nothing about, so it is easier to channel your worry into something more productive.

● Track your stressors by keeping a journal for 5-7 days to identify which situations create the most stress and how you tend to respond to each situation.

● Establish boundaries with co-workers when controlling the work-related activities you undertake.

● Learn how to gauge your stress signals because it is a good first step to managing stress. Examples of stress signals include having a hard time concentrating or making decisions, feeling irritable or out of control, having muscle tension, or lacking energy.

Activity 17.1 (continued)

Answers available at end of chapter.

● Practice mindfulness—focus completely on everything you are doing now to feel calmer and happier.

● Reach out to a loved one—leaning on those you trust for advice, comfort, and reassurance helps lessen stress levels.

? If you were to choose from the above activities, which two seem to work best for you in times of stress? Why?

EXAMPLE OF BEST PRACTICES
Stress Management
https://www.bizjournals.com/bizjournals/how-to/ growth-strategies/2017/07/8-ways-employers-can- minimize-workplace-stress.html *Accessed 6/11/2018*

Workplace stress is the basis for thousands of work-stress illness claims being filed in courts throughout the United States. The following are ways a company can support employees to minimize workplace stress.

- Nothing causes stress to an employee like poor management, so providing proper training to supervisors on employee management is important.

- Provide conflict resolution training to assist employees who are in difficult work situations with other employees.

- Do not tolerate workplace bullying—immediately identify the behavior, name it, and deal with it.

- Establish policies that support emotional wellness and treatment and create a culture of support for those who ask for help.

- Consider a corporate wellness program to promote employees' self-care. Such a program can address a healthier diet, exercise, tobacco cessation, depression education, and financial resources to assist in debt management and retirement planning.

 ## Soft Skills Tip 17.1
Stress arises when you perceive a situation as demanding. For example, your morning commute may make you anxious and tense because you worry that traffic will make you late. Others may find the trip relaxing because it allows more time to enjoy music or quiet time.

 ## Soft Skills Tip 17.2
If you cannot discuss your feelings within your support network (e.g., family or friends), then express them some other way—such as writing about them in a journal or composing a letter and simply not mailing it.

 # Activity 17.2

Answers available at end of chapter.

This exercise provides you a process to cope with your personal stress. With a recent stressor in mind, use these three steps to take better control of your situation.

1. Identify the factors that cause stress in your life so you can change or better manage them.

2. Make a list of the situations, relationships, and events that are stressful for you.

3. Once you have a stress awareness checklist, you can begin to make decisions about which ones need immediate attention.

# FURTHER RESEARCH AND PRETEST LINKS

American Psychological Association: Stress
http://www.apa.org/topics/stress/index.aspx

Pretest by 15Minutes4Me.com
https://www.15minutes4me.com/free-online-test-stress-anxiety-depression-burnout/

Answers to Chapter 17 Exercises

Note: Though answers may vary due to experience and previous training, the following are suggested responses.

Activity 17.1: Student responses will vary relative which activities work best for them to relieve stress in their lives.

Activity 17.2: Student responses will vary relative the stressors they are currently dealing with in their lives.

Choices 17.1: Asking for a raise is stressful, to be sure. In most cases, the person doesn't want the embarrassment of being turned down for the raise. However, if you follow the suggestions given in this situation, you have at least given the conversation with your boss a good try and paved the way for a later pay raise.

NOTES:

CHAPTER 18
Professional Awareness

"The ultimate value of life depends upon awareness and the power of contemplation rather than upon mere survival."
Aristotle, Greek Philosopher

✅ SOME EXAMPLES OF PROFESSIONAL AWARENESS

- Consulting your local community college's class schedule to see what economical one-day, business-related workshops are offered next semester.

- Making a birthday promise to yourself to stay fit by exercising regularly and eating more healthy foods over the coming year.

- Periodically going through your closet to ensure the clothes you wear on the job are workday ready—meaning, they are clean and pressed, stain- and odor-free, and not ripped or torn.

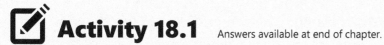 **Activity 18.1** Answers available at end of chapter.

Describe two encounters you've had recently with people who demonstrated:
- ◆ poor etiquette or manners, and
- ◆ good etiquette or manners

? Contrast the impressions you were left with in both situations. Why are impressions by customers, suppliers, and distributors important in business settings?

Professional Awareness

A composite system composed of images, beliefs, thoughts, feelings, behaviors, and attitudes which are inherent in the individual as well as within a specific profession.

💡 Soft Skills Tip 18.1

Respect is at the heart of good manners. All good manners are based on thoughtfulness for others and respect for them as individuals of equal value.

💡 Soft Skills Tip 18.2

Remember that you never get a second chance to make a first impression.

⚠ KEEP THESE POINTS IN MIND ABOUT PROFESSIONAL AWARENESS

- One of the most effective ways to deal with change is to pursue lifelong learning, because it helps you avoid stagnation and reach your full potential. Also, the more you learn, the better you will become at seeing more sides of the same situation—helping you understand more deeply and make better decisions.

- Learning new things gives us a feeling of accomplishment, which in turn boosts our confidence in our capabilities. For example, to function effectively in this rapidly changing world of technology, you need to learn new methods and devices to remain valuable on the job.

- Be aware of what your work associate is doing when you approach his or her desk. If the person is clearly in the middle of something, ask if you can schedule a time to chat; don't just start talking.

- While it may feel as if you are being especially efficient by answering emails during a conference call, the reality is that you are likely creating more work for yourself since you are not truly concentrating on either task well.

- Good manners and etiquette contribute to a positive first and lasting impression in social and business situations, as well as give you a favorable reputation.

- Dressing appropriately and being well-groomed make a positive statement about you and your employer.

- Listen to podcasts and watch TED videos as a type of "free cyber training" for continuous learning opportunities.

- It's not necessary to shout to colleagues over the top of your cubicle. Walk over to the person you want to talk to, call them on the phone, or send an e-mail.

- Take care how and when you use your mobile devices, and do not use them at inappropriate times (e.g., while driving, in meetings, when engaged in conversation with another person).

- Prior to your first day on the job, contact the Human Resource Department to see if the company you are working for has a dress code for employees.

EXAMPLE OF BEST PRACTICES
Professional Awareness
http://news.gallup.com/businessjournal/189212/
attracts-best-employees-company.aspx
Accessed 6/8/2018

When leaders see their best performers achieve business outcomes, they no doubt wish they could get more similarly talented people to apply to and join their company.

Here's an example of an effective Employee Value Proposition from Apple in action: When Apple added full education reimbursement for workers to its list of employee perks, some onlookers might have said, "What an extraordinary investment in their employees," or "What a great way to develop their workforce and to retain talented employees." But in Silicon Valley, those directly involved in the hunt for top talent realized that in the same way that Apple creates innovative new products, it had created an attraction strategy that differentiated the company from its competitors—and that appealed directly to the type of employee it wanted to hire. Apple's brilliantly defined employment brand not only speaks to people with a strong desire to learn and grow, but also says a lot about the company's culture and what it values.

 # Choices 18.1

It's the third time this month that Lucy has come to work wearing much-too-casual attire (some say they look like her *pajamas*). You, as her supervisor, are beginning to reach the end of your rope and feel you cannot put off any longer saying something to her, as it appears to be affecting her co-workers' attention and performance on the job. You want your employees—especially the most recently hired millennials, like Lucy—to be happy, but you also don't want the office to lose any or all sense of decorum and professionalism.

? So what are you to do?

? Specifically, how would you approach your discussion with Lucy and then script what you would say during your meeting with her?

Answers available at end of chapter.

 **Activity 18.2**

Answers available at end of chapter.

Assume the company you work for gives employees a $1,000 educational stipend each year to further their learning and growth on the job. Employees may choose to pay for a community college class, a professional seminar, or a conference registration fee, among other opportunities.

? How would you research training opportunities in your city?

? Which training option would you select, and why?

? Do you think this is a good benefit that companies should use to professionally advance workers on the job or toward a new position? Discuss.

 FURTHER RESEARCH AND PRETEST LINKS

Association for Talent Development

https://www.td.org/magazines/td-magazine/10-ways-to-build-a-culture-of-continuous-learning

Pretest by AARP

https://www.aarp.org/work/on-the-job/info-09-2012/good-office-manners-quiz.html#quest2

Answers to Chapter 18 Exercises

Note: Though answers may vary due to experience and previous training, the following are suggested responses.

Activity 18.1: Student responses will vary but it is extremely important to demonstrate good manners and etiquette because first impressions are lasting ones.

Activity 18.2: Student responses will vary. Conducting research as to training opportunities in your community is an important first step to advancing professionally on the job.

Choices 18.1: This is a tricky situation. It requires you to have a feeling about just how much pressure to put on Lucy when addressing the appropriateness of her dress in the workplace. Be sure to focus your comments on the effect Lucy's clothing is having on co-workers' productivity, not on Lucy per se.

NOTES:

About the Author

Dr. Pattie Gibson has taught courses in customer service, computer applications, business management, office systems, and educational administration and technology to university, community college, and high school students in Colorado, Arizona, and Germany. She received her bachelor's and master's degrees from Arizona State University and her doctorate from Northern Arizona University.

Her business experience has progressed through a wide range of positions, from student secretary while in college to trainer and manager for IBM® to sales representative for both IBM and Papermate/Gillette® corporations on both the East and West coasts. In addition to teaching, she served as Dean of Instruction at Coconino Community College in Flagstaff and later as a tenured professor at Northern Arizona University. Over the years and continuing to this day, she operates a successful computer and customer service consulting and training business in Colorado, where she resides.

Dr. Gibson, a nationally recognized speaker at business and educational conferences, is also a published author of seven other textbooks, including *The World of Customer Service, Administrative Office Management, Modern Office Procedures,* and *Office Skills.* She enjoys interacting with present and former students, traveling, reading, and spending time with family and friends. She has a grown daughter and son—each of whom are exceptionally good and accomplished people.

CPSIA information can be obtained
at www.ICGtesting.com
Printed in the USA
LVHW061454070621
689564LV00008B/518